# MAKERS

*of the*

# CARIBBEAN

**Photo Credits**

The following photos are courtesy of the National Library of Jamaica:
Norman Manley, p. 23
Alexander Bustamante, pp. 34, 35.
Marcus Garvey, p. 47
Claude McKay, p. 71
Louise Bennett, p. 89
Edna Manley, pp. 106, 107

The following photos are courtesy of the Ministry of Public Administration
and Information, Trinidad:
C.L.R. James, p. 53
Eric Williams, p. 61

The following photos are courtesy of Jerry A. Sierra (www.historyofcuba.com)
Antonio Maceo, pp. 10,12
José Martí, p. 45

Photo of Enriquillo p. 3 courtesy of Roger Atihuibancex Hernandez of the
United Confederation of Taino People (www.uctp.org)

Photo of Nanny p. 5 courtesy of the Jamaica National Heritage Trust

Photo of Jean-Jacques Dessalines p. 17 courtesy of www.wehaitians.com

Photo of Errol Barrow p. 28 courtesy of the Democratic Labour Party, Barbados

Photo of Jacques Roumain p. 76 courtesy of the Centre International de
Documentation et d'Information Hatienne, Caraibéenne et Afro-Canadienne (CIDIHCA)

Photo of Louise Bennett p. 88 by Maria LaYacona

Photo of Wifredo Lam p. 109 and painting 'La Silla' p. 110 © ADAGP, Paris 2004

Photo of the Mighty Sparrow p.117 courtesy of the Ministry of Information and
Communications Technology, Trinidad

Photo of Bob Marley p. 120 courtesy of the Jamaica Information Service

Photo of Roberto Clemente p. 133 courtesy of the Baseball Hall of Fame Library,
Cooperstown, NY.

Photos of Sir Garfield Sobers pp. 135, 137 courtesy of the Barbados Information Service.

# MAKERS
## *of the*
# CARIBBEAN

## James Ferguson

Institut
de Coopération
Franco Caraïbe

*Guadeloupe*

**Ian Randle Publishers**
*Kingston* ● *Miami*

Published 2005, by
Ian Randle Publishers
11 Cunningham Avenue
Box 686
Kingston 6, Jamaica
www.ianrandlepublishers.com

and the

Institut de Coopération  Franco Caraïbe
Cite des Metiers – av. Du General deGaulle
Raizet – 97139 ABYMES
Guadeloupe, French West Indies

National Library of Jamaica Cataloguing in Publication Data

Ferguson, James
    Makers of the Caribbean /  James Ferguson

        p.;    cm

    Bibliography : p.


    ISBN 976-637-003-6



    1. Caribbean Area – History       2.   Caribbean Area - Culture
    3. Caribbean Area – Intellectual life


    972.9          dc 21

Cover and book design by Robert Harris
Set in Veracity 10.5/14.5 x 35

Printed in the United States of America

# CONTENTS

# PREFACE

At a time when individuals and institutions in the French-speaking Caribbean are showing a particular interest in books covering the history and culture of their region, it seemed appropriate to try to meet this need by putting at their disposal a work that deals with this vast subject in a condensed form.

With this in mind, we found James Ferguson's book *Makers of the Caribbean* extremely suitable, as the personalities and themes it discusses cast considerable light on the cultural history of the Caribbean. Dr Ferguson, formerly of Oxford University and a researcher at London's Latin America Bureau, looks at a range of individuals, both historic and contemporary, as illustrations of the region's diversity and cultural creativity.

This led the Institute of French Caribbean Cooperation, with the support of the Regional Council of Guadeloupe, the Prefecture of Guadeloupe and its Regional Office for Cultural Affairs, to undertake the coordination and translation of the French version of this book, leaving its Jamaican publisher, Ian Randle, in charge of its distribution.

In the following pages most of us will find a good deal of information on almost all of the Greater and Lesser Antilles through the exceptional individuals, men and women, who have lived there. Whether in the field of history, literature, the visual arts, music or sports, we will come to discover, sometimes to our surprise, that our Caribbean compatriots have had a significant impact on contemporary culture and have also greatly contributed to world history.

This book should help us to know our region better, especially its human dimension. By gaining insights into our neighbours' history and culture, as shaped through the centuries, we are better able to understand them, their attitudes, their aspirations, and what binds all Caribbean people together in a shared experience.

Easy to read, this book is accessible to all – scholars, students, the public at large – and it renders a true account of Caribbean society, its development through the centuries, and its considerable contribution to the modern world.

This book has much to offer. I hope that it will be warmly received.

**Max Vincent**
President of the Institut de Coopération Franco Caraïbe

# INTRODUCTION

In 1962, the Trinidad-born author V.S. Naipaul dismissed the entirety of the Caribbean's history in a few bad-tempered words. Writing in *The Middle Passage*, he remarked that 'history is built around achievement and creation, and nothing was created in the West Indies.' The book, a dyspeptic account of Naipaul's travels through English, French and Dutch-speaking territories, also carried as epigraph a quotation from *The English in the West Indies* by James Anthony Froude, which ends: 'There are no people there in the true sense of the word, with a character and purpose of their own.'

Could Naipaul have really meant that the Caribbean and its people have never created anything? Could he have approved of the arch-imperialist Froude's proposal that these same people are without character or purpose? If so, it is an extraordinary assessment of a part of the world, scarred by slavery and saddled with the heavy legacy of the plantation system, yet constantly inventive, creative and – unlike Naipaul's dour dismissal – irrepressibly positive. When Naipaul was writing, the Cuban Revolution was in its infancy, the Missile Crisis about to break. This was history in the making, yet the writer chose to ignore it. Another revolution, that which created the independent state of Haiti in 1804, had already marked a unique moment in history, the one and only occasion when a slave rebellion succeeded in overthrowing the colonial order and replacing it with independent nationhood. This, too, was not counted by Naipaul, or his predecessor Froude, as significant history.

Naipaul was, of course, writing in the early 1960s, before the advent of independence in most Caribbean territories, at a time that predated the boom in Caribbean literature, the worldwide impact of reggae music, the golden age of West Indies cricket. But even so, his charge that the region had created nothing seems as absurd now as it must have done to readers then. Blinded by his own elitist conception of what achievement and creation might entail, Naipaul was unable to recognise that Caribbean creativity cannot be measured by European, classical criteria, that achievement is not the exclusive preserve of 'greats' such as Michelangelo or Mozart. Instead, the region's cultural richness resides precisely in its popular forms of art, music and self-expression, in qualities such as inventiveness, adaptation and openness. The steelband music that Naipaul admitted to detesting is a case in point.

Born seemingly fortuitously by a curious hand tapping a rhythm on an old oil drum, it has grown to become one of the most appreciated of popular musical forms, a sound that is at once specifically evocative of Carnival and yet infinitely versatile.

Great music has come from the mean ghettos of inner-city Kingston. Great painting has been produced by illiterate peasants from remote villages in Haiti. Great literature has been written by those who grew up in homes without books. Individuals who wanted to create or compete in the Caribbean have often had to do so without the resources of those in wealthier parts of the world. The desire to excel has often been joined to a fierce determination to overcome every sort of hurdle, not least those of poverty and discrimination. This is why resourcefulness has often played such an important part in Caribbean success stories.

But what truly distances the vibrancy of Caribbean culture from Naipaul's sterile definition is not simply its resilience, but its ability and willingness to embrace the many influences – linguistic, artistic, technical – that make up the region's identity. For this is an area marked by massive migration, much of it forced, by the coming together of people from Africa, India, China and Europe in New World societies characterised by diversity and difference. The forming of a truly Creole culture was achieved not by dismissing some forms and canonising others, but by the synthesis and adaptation of what was most relevant to people living in these societies. Hence, unique forms of communication and cultural expression came into being, as differing traditions and aesthetics collided, merged and metamorphosed.

It is in the spirit of a riposte to Naipaul's judgment that this book is intended. It aims to show that the Caribbean, far from being a place without history and creativity, is alive with both. Its history is remembered and recorded in many different ways, but I have sought to make at least episodes of it accessible by concentrating on key individuals who played a determining part in the process. In the same way, I hope that looking at the lives and achievements of selected writers, artists and musicians will give some indication of the wider picture, of their work in a broader context. These forty-seven individuals, ranging from indigenous freedom fighter to modern-day athlete, stand as evidence of the Caribbean's historic and cultural significance.

Many of these figures, historical and contemporary, are of interest because they are clearly exceptional. A Marcus Garvey or Fidel Castro, for example, are not ordinary individuals by any definition. But others I have chosen because they are more typical than exceptional, or because they represent to an unusual degree a facet of Caribbean history or culture. Needless to say, this process of selection has not been an easy one and I am sure that many readers will disagree with my choice. I am particularly conscious that women are heavily outnumbered by men in this collection of profiles. This, I suggest, is largely because *machismo* is not a purely Hispanic phenomenon and because women have long been excluded or marginalised from prominence in public life. Few women have reached the top echelons of politics in any Caribbean society, and with the exception of literature the creative arts have also been dominated by men. Fortunately, this situation is now changing, with a majority of graduates from the

University of the West Indies, for instance, being women. Should a book of this sort appear at the beginning of the next century, it will doubtless be very different in its gender balance.

As anyone who has spent time in Haiti, rural Jamaica or indeed any Caribbean island will know, women are normally the real force behind day-to-day life, behind the local economy and community life. That is why a book of this sort, by selecting a number of more or less famous individuals, can only ever hope to give a partial picture of how the Caribbean has become what it is today. In this sense, the real makers of the Caribbean are the unsung and often anonymous people whose lives may be largely undocumented but whose strengths and talents have shaped the region's development. 'Great men' (and women) should act, therefore, more as signposts, as human milestones in the long process of self-emancipation and creativity which, despite Naipaul's evaluation, has made up the Caribbean's fascinating and often heroic history.

James Ferguson
May 2004

# THE FIGHT FOR FREEDOM

*Enriquillo*

(Dominican Republic)

*Nanny*

(Jamaica)

*Toussaint L'Ouverture*

(Haiti)

*Antonio Maceo*

(Cuba)

*Louis Delgrès*

(Guadeloupe)

The Caribbean's long and turbulent history is marked by the continuous search for freedom. Freedom from slavery, freedom from political oppression, freedom from poverty. The burden of foreign interference, of colonial exploitation has lain heavily on the region since the first arrival of Europeans in 1492, and much of the fight for freedom has revolved around casting off that burden.

Resistance to colonial power began almost with the first landfall of Christopher Columbus. The odds against the peaceable indigenous Tainos were overwhelming, however, and their extinction rapidly became inevitable. Yet some exceptional individuals are still remembered for their spirited opposition to the Spanish occupation. Queen Anacaona was hanged by the *conquistadores* for daring to question their presence in her land. Hatuey, a cacique or chieftain, refused to be baptised when awaiting execution, for he understood that in the European's version of heaven he might meet yet more Spaniards.

The imposition of slavery and the development of the plantation system created violent and artificial societies, in which the privileged few literally lived from the sweat of the many. Slavery bred hatred and revolt as surely as it made vast profits for the planters and their European merchant allies. It also sharpened an almost unbearable thirst for freedom, and there were many who sought escape, either through running away or through fighting the hated oppressor. In each large island where there were remote mountains and wild interiors, escaped slaves formed communities, defending themselves against recapture and living by their wits and by hunting. Known in English as Maroons, they became powerful forces, able to terrify the colonial authorities into allowing them their autonomy in return for an end to raiding. Alongside the legendary Nanny were formidable figures such as the brothers

1

Accompong and Cudjoe, who led a long fight against the British in Jamaica until a treaty was signed in 1739. Their descendants still live in the town of Accompong in the inaccessible Cockpit Country.

Full-scale rebellion was another option, and the history of the eighteenth-century Caribbean is punctuated by slave revolts and, in most cases, savage reprisals. There were several important uprisings in Jamaica, in Cuba and in Antigua. In 1763 the mainland Dutch colony of Berbice (now part of Guyana) witnessed an overwhelming insurrection, led by a slave called Coffy, which was put down only when warships and reinforcements from Barbados arrived. Even the tiny Danish-ruled island of St John was rocked by an uprising in 1733, during which the slaves massacred many white colonists. There were, of course, individual leaders such as Tacky and Sam Sharpe in Jamaica or Bussa in Barbados, but many thousands of unknown or anonymous slaves also risked everything in desperate attempts to overthrow the system that held them in bondage.

Only one slave revolt eventually evolved into a successful revolution, as the jewel in the French empire's crown, Saint Domingue, collapsed under the weight of slave resistance, foreign meddling and yellow fever. The birth of Haiti terrified slave-owners throughout the Americas and hastened the end of slavery. It also immortalised the figure of Toussaint L'Ouverture, born a slave but rising to challenge the military might of Napoleon Bonaparte himself.

Haiti's traumatic independence was the first in the Caribbean or Latin America, and many more fights ensued against the colonial powers. Perhaps none in the Caribbean was as bitter as Cuba's struggle to end Spanish rule. It took two extended wars for the Spanish to be dislodged from their 'pearl of the Antilles', and it took the courage and skill of fighters such as Antonio Maceo and the Dominican Máximo Gómez to win a conflict against all the odds.

Independence has not in every case led to freedom, and modern Caribbean history has produced many guerrillas and other fighters who have struggled against what they saw as tyranny. Most revolts and uprisings have ended in failure or apathy – Trinidad's Black Power rebellion in 1970, the short-lived Grenadian revolution, many popular revolts against price rises or government cutbacks – but one in particular, Fidel Castro's audacious campaign against the Batista dictatorship, ended in victory and changed the face of the Caribbean.

For most people in the Caribbean today, fundamental freedoms can be more or less taken for granted. The Commonwealth Caribbean has a solid record of democratic elections and participation, and few islands experience overt censorship or political repression. Those territories, still under some sort of European or US tutelage, have found enough autonomy to satisfy the majority of their people. Only Cuba and Haiti in their very different ways remain outside the common mould of stable parliamentary democracy.

The freedoms that people long for now are the freedom to live without fear of illness, poverty or old age, or the freedom to migrate in search of a better life.

The Sierra Bahoruco mountain range rises steep and densely wooded near the Dominican Republic's border with Haiti. Today it is a protected national park, a wild and remote haven for birds and pine forests. But nearly 500 years ago, this was the scene of one of the last and most important rebellions against Spanish colonial rule by the region's indigenous Taino people.

The Tainos had inhabited the larger islands of the Caribbean for hundreds of years before the arrival of Christopher Columbus in 1492. They lived in large villages, governed by *caciques* or chieftains, subsisted on fishing and farming and were accomplished potters. Peaceful by nature, the Tainos on the island Columbus was to name Hispaniola numbered anywhere between 100,000 and a million.

The arrival of the Europeans was a catastrophe for these gentle people. Forced to hunt for gold, abused and exploited, they quickly succumbed to European diseases like smallpox or sheer mistreatment. The Spanish conquerors divided them up in the so-called *encomienda* system, allotting whole communities as serfs to the new European landowners. The Tainos had little choice but to work like slaves, facing torture and execution if they failed to cooperate.

# ENRIQUILLO
## 1500?–1535
### DOMINICAN REPUBLIC

But one *cacique*, known only by the Spanish name of Enriquillo, was not prepared to bow to the inevitable. We know little about his early life, other than he was the orphaned son of a Taino chieftain, probably murdered by the Spanish, and that he became *cacique* in his turn. His fiefdom was Jaragua, an area in the centre of the island. He was educated under the auspices of Spanish Franciscan friars at the Monasterio San Francisco, from where he emerged more literate and articulate than most of the uneducated *conquistadores* who controlled the island. It is said that he spoke perfect Spanish and had read widely in history, philosophy and theology. He was also baptised as a Christian.

After this privileged interlude, however, Enriquillo was expected to work under the *encomienda* system, and he was sent to the Jaragua region to ensure that his community toiled for the local landowner. What happened next is unclear, but legend has it that Enriquillo's wife was abused and almost raped by a Spaniard, Andrés de Valenzuela, and that the *cacique* swore to take revenge. Seeking justice first from the colony's governor and then from the Real Audiencia, the royal judiciary, he received no recompense and was even threatened with imprisonment. In 1519, having exhausted all legal options, he escaped from the *encomienda* with several hundred followers and established a base high in the Sierra Bahoruco.

By now, the Taino population was a fraction of what it had been before the arrival of Columbus. In January 1519, a lethal epidemic of smallpox had swept through the indigenous population, leaving perhaps only 3,000 Taino survivors. Enriquillo's band of rebels were among this small minority, and their isolation in the remote mountains probably helped them escape the disease. Gradually, other small groups of Tainos heard of his escape and joined the rebels. Over time, the runaway community grew to about 2,000, including women and children.

As a local revolt began to develop into a full-scale insurrection, the colonial authorities tried to capture Enriquillo and destroy his rebel hideout. Four separate expeditions were launched to hunt him down, but all failed because of the impenetrable mountain terrain and the resistance of Enriquillo's warriors. Arming themselves only with what weapons they could steal from the Spanish, his warriors carried out deadly hit-and-run raids on their pursuers. They also allied themselves with other runaways in the mountains, the *cimarrones* or escaped black slaves, who from the beginning of African slavery in the early 1520s had sought refuge in the island's wilderness. As their confidence grew, the rebels launched attacks on plantations and settlements in the fertile plains, stealing livestock and arms.

For 14 years Enriquillo and his followers held out in the mountains, out of reach of the Spanish forces. According to one version of events, in a particularly audacious raid they even attacked a gold-laden galleon in the harbour at Barahona, helping themselves to its cargo. Eventually the Spanish realised that mere force of arms would not conquer the last *cacique* and they sent emissaries, including priests, to negotiate with the rebels. After lengthy discussions, the head of the Spanish armed forces, Hernando de San Martín, signed a peace treaty with Enriquillo. The document, dated 1533 and signed by the Spanish King Carlos I, pledged that the remaining Tainos would be spared from further forced labour and that they would be settled on a reservation.

The Spanish kept their part of the bargain, and Enriquillo was provided with a suitable house near Azua, where he died in 1535, apparently from tuberculosis contracted during his gruelling years in the mountains. The other Tainos were given land near what is today called Lago Enriquillo, the huge inland saltwater lake near the border with Haiti. They lived no longer than another two decades before dying out, either from smallpox or despair at the loss of their old way of life. By 1550 there were no Tainos left alive on the island of Hispaniola.

In 1882, a Dominican writer and politician Manuel Jesús de Galván resurrected the legend of the last *cacique* in his novel *Enriquillo*. Galván depicted the Taino rebel as an archetypal romantic 'noble savage', at odds with a corrupt colonial society and embodying a timeless thirst for freedom. As a Spanish-speaking, Christianised character, he was also a perfect hero for a nation that looked to Spain for its cultural heritage and tended to despise neighbouring Haiti with its African-inspired traditions. The novel struck a chord with Dominican readers, who liked to see in the inspiring figure of Enriquillo a symbolic founding father figure. Ignoring the fact that almost all Dominicans are of mixed European and African ancestry, it became fashionable to claim Taino parentage, and even nowadays mixed-race Dominicans tend to refer to themselves as *indios*. Enriquillo, whose name is remembered today with the lake, a town and a province, accordingly became a celebrated figure in Dominican history, representing an ideal fusion between a European model of civilisation and a distant indigenous past.

The history of slavery and of the plantation system is also the history of those who resisted servitude. Resistance took many forms, not least the many rebellions and insurrections which punctuated colonial Caribbean history from the seventeenth century to the arrival of emancipation. But perhaps the most romanticised of slavery's enemies were the Maroons, runaway groups and communities of men, women and children who escaped the horrors of slavery for a precarious, but free existence on the wild margins of colonial society.

# NANNY
## 1680?–1750?
JAMAICA

Maroons (the term is an anglicised corruption of the Spanish word *cimarrón*, meaning wild or untamed) existed in most New World territories where there was space enough for them to set up their outlaw communities. In small, flat Barbados, for instance, such an enterprise would have been unthinkable, but in Hispaniola, in mountainous islands like Dominica and St Vincent, and in the jungle expanses of Suriname, large, autonomous Maroon settlements took root. Jamaica was home to arguably the most famous of these fugitive groups, and it was in the high peaks of the Blue Mountains and the inhospitable wilderness of the Cockpit Country that they established their free villages.

Jamaica's Maroons owe their existence, paradoxically, to the English takeover of the island in 1655. Until then, the island had been a Spanish possession, a sparsely populated and largely neglected outpost of Spain's empire. The ranchers and tobacco farmers imported African slaves from 1517 onwards to replace the rapidly dwindling Taino population, but this was far from the labour-intensive plantation system of later centuries. When the English arrived, the fleeing Spaniards set their slaves free, urging them to take to the mountains and harry the new occupants of the island. Given the opportunity to fend for themselves, the freed slaves promptly established themselves in some of the island's most inaccessible areas.

Only one year after the English capture of Jamaica, Major-General Robert Sedgwick complained that these runaway slaves were already 'a thorn in the side of the English'. Raiding and robbing the fledgling English settlements, they were a serious menace. 'There scarce a week passeth without one or two slain by them', wrote Sedgwick, 'and as we grow secure, they grow bold and bloody.' Some, such as Juan de Bolas, were tempted by English offers of peace, but he was murdered by other rebels, outraged at his treachery. And so it remained for another century, as the Maroons consolidated their presence in the Blue Mountains and Cockpit Country. Those in the eastern mountains were known as the Windward Maroons, while those based in the western Cockpit Country were called the Leeward Maroons.

The ranks of the rebels gradually swelled as slaves escaped from the expanding English-owned plantations. Some escaped as soon as they had arrived in the island, while others took years to make their decision. Occasionally, a Maroon raiding party would descend on a plantation, capture food, animals and arms, and liberate slaves, particularly women. Children were born in the Maroon villages, keeping up the communities' numbers. Maroons were also famed for their longevity, with many apparently living to a hundred or older. For these reasons, these communities survived.

War with the British finally broke out in 1690, when a number of slaves in the parish of Clarendon, mostly warlike Coromantees from Africa's Gold Coast, escaped and joined forces with the established Maroons. For several decades a simmering guerrilla war occasionally boiled up into pitched battles, especially from 1724 onwards, with the Maroons fighting a devastating hit-and-run warfare against the terrified British. Commanding these feared fighters were their leaders, the Maroon elders, many of whom were women.

Today, the most revered of these female freedom fighters is Nanny, a part historical, part mythical figure, whose tantalisingly incomplete life-story merely adds to her general mystique. Official, written history has little to say about this woman, who was reputed to be the tactical genius and spiritual force behind the Maroons' successful resistance. But oral history, still recounted in today's Maroon communities, remembers her as a pivotal figure in the fight against colonial oppression.

We know nothing certain about Nanny's early years, nor about her arrival in Jamaica. She was reputed to have been born of noble blood in what is today Ghana. More implausibly, it is claimed by some that she was never a slave, that she either came to Jamaica as a free person or that she escaped as soon as her ship arrived. In any case, oral history suggests that this woman, commonly known as Queen Nanny, was a powerful figure among the Windward Maroons during the time of the war with the British. She was, it seems, married to a man named Adou, and, improbably, was the sister of other famed Maroon leaders such as Cudjoe, Accompong and Quao.

None of the above can be supported by historical evidence, but folk culture insists that Nanny was a powerful military leader as well as a symbol of the resilience of African culture. She was instrumental in perfecting the use of the *abeng*, the symbol of Maroon resistance. This cow's horn, like an African talking drum, was used by skilled horn blowers to transmit information over long distances in a code that the British troops could never understand. Their arrival could be announced by lookouts hours before they actually materialised, enabling escape or ambushes to be organised. Nanny is also credited with developing the Maroons' sophisticated use of camouflage, a technique that allowed them to ambush the red-coated British forces with a devastating element of surprise. Legend even has it that she possessed supernatural powers that enabled her to catch British bullets (one vulgar version claims between her buttocks!) and fire them back at the astonished soldiers. This and other stories support the supposition that she practised *obeah*, the African-descended mixture of magic and spirituality that is still part of Jamaican popular culture.

This fierce woman's qualities were so appreciated by her fellow Maroons that a mountain settlement was named after her, Nanny Town. This place was the site of one of the few British victories in the long war against the Maroons, for it was here that a

Captain Stoddart managed to drag some small artillery up the mountains and fire down onto the huts below. Many villagers were reported dead and the settlement was abandoned and never repopulated. Today, only a collection of strange overgrown shapes remains, and Nanny Town is believed to be haunted. The surviving Maroons moved to a village they called Moore Town, which is where their descendants still live today.

The war finally came to an end in 1739 when the British signed a treaty with Cudjoe, leader of the Leeward Maroons. The following year, Quao signed a similar treaty on behalf of the Windward Maroons, agreeing to cease hostilities in return for a grant of land and guaranteed autonomy. The Maroons also agreed to return any new runaway slaves to their masters – a condition that has caused much controversy ever since.

Interestingly, the name of Nanny does not appear in any of the papers surrounding the truce. Did she disapprove of it? Or was she dead by then? It seems that she was alive, for in 1740 a royal decree was published which stated:

> George the 2nd by the Grace of God of Great Britain, France and Ireland and King of Jamaica, Lord Defender of the Faith . . . have given and granted . . . and do give and grant unto Nanny and the people residing with her and other heirs and I do assign a certain parcel of land containing five hundred acres in the parish of Portland branching north south east on Kingsland . . .

Thereafter, nothing is heard of this mysterious woman warrior. It is only a guess that she died at some point in the 1750s. But her memory lived on among the Maroons, who told stories about her valour and supernatural powers. In 1976, the Jamaican government finally named her as a national hero, and each year in October, on National Heroes' Day, Maroons and others gather to honour Nanny's memory to the sound of *abeng* horns and Coromantee drums.

*A Jamaican five hundred dollar bill featuring Nanny*

# TOUSSAINT L'OUVERTURE
## 1746?–1803
### HAITI

The leader of the only successful slave revolution in history, Toussaint L'Ouverture played a vital role not just in the creation of the independent state of Haiti, but also in the ending of slavery throughout the western hemisphere. His military and political skills were instrumental in freeing half a million slaves from captivity and building a new nation. His greatest failing, however, was to believe that he could cooperate with the former French colonial masters, and this led to his tragic downfall.

Born a slave in the French colony of Saint Domingue, Toussaint Bréda (Bréda was the name of his master's plantation) was reputedly the eldest son of an African chieftain who had been captured and enslaved. He enjoyed a relatively privileged youth under a liberal master and even received some education from another slave, Pierre Baptiste, who taught him to read. Toussaint became coachman to his master and then steward of all the plantation livestock. He was a trusted and well-treated member of the plantation's workforce, but nevertheless a slave.

In the 1780s, Saint Domingue was the most prosperous colony in the Caribbean and the world, containing hundreds of sugar plantations and exporting huge amounts of sugar, coffee and cocoa back to France. But it was also a place where the vast majority of black slaves were treated inhumanely, where lives were short and brutal, where revolution was inevitable. Several abortive plots and uprisings took place in the second half of the eighteenth century; all were suppressed with great brutality by the colonial authorities.

Legend has it that Toussaint was present at the voodoo ceremony which began the slave uprising in the north of the colony in August 1791. It is also believed that he helped his master to escape to safety before the violence broke out. The revolt followed on the heels of the French Revolution two years earlier, which had inspired the slaves with its ideas of liberty, equality and fraternity. Carefully organised by a secret leadership, the uprising took the white planters and the island militia by surprise. The loss of life and damage to plantations were unlike anything ever seen before in the Caribbean. At the same time, further revolts and fighting broke out elsewhere in Saint Domingue.

The revolutionary government in France sent a force of 6,000 men to attempt to pacify the colony, but by now Spanish troops from the western side of the island, Santo Domingo, and British troops had become involved. Fighting alongside the Spanish, some slaves hoped to force the French into granting them their freedom. This tactic succeeded and in August 1793, the French commissioners, sent over by the revolutionary government in Paris, decreed the abolition of slavery.

At this point, under the leadership of Toussaint, the slaves suddenly changed sides, attacking both the Spanish and British forces. Toussaint had heard that in Paris the government had officially confirmed the abolition of slavery and he now wanted to drive the reactionary Spanish and British out of the island. By now, Toussaint was famed as a military leader. Nicknamed L'Ouverture ('the opening' in French) because he could always find gaps in the enemy ranks, he was in charge of an army of former slaves who practised a devastating form of hit-and-run guerrilla warfare. Descending quickly from the mountains or staging murderous ambushes, they struck terror into their opponents' hearts. His troops, Toussaint said, were 'as naked as earthworms', but they managed to drive the Spanish back into their own colony and force the British to abandon their invasion. Ravaged by yellow fever, the British were forced to give up their dream of seizing Saint Domingue.

By 1800, Toussaint was undisputed master of the island, and the following year he proclaimed himself governor-general of the colony for life. Under his rule, the economy began to recover, the former slaves returned as free labourers to the plantations, exports of coffee and sugar resumed. But Toussaint was a harsh ruler, tolerating no dissent. With an army of 20,000, he forced his people back to work. He also handed out large tracts of land to his top-ranking officers, encouraging them to become involved in the export economy. Some white planters returned to their properties, and Toussaint sought to establish friendly relations with them.

The colony's recovery was no comfort to Napoleon Bonaparte who had come to power in France and swore to remove Toussaint and reintroduce slavery. Although Saint Domingue was still nominally a French colony, it was apparent that Toussaint was very much in charge, and this hurt Napoleon's pride. He resolved to reimpose his will on the colony and dispatched a fleet, commanded by his brother-in-law, General Leclerc, to re-establish French rule. After the enormous expedition of 22,000 men arrived in late 1801, conflict soon broke out and Toussaint led resistance to the French reoccupation. But the odds were overwhelming and Toussaint gave up the fight, perhaps waiting for yellow fever to destroy the French as it had the British. Toussaint was by nature a negotiator, somebody who believed that he could win his cause through compromise and collaboration.

In June 1802, Toussaint was invited to a meeting with the French commander, seized and shipped off to France, where he was imprisoned in a freezing fortress in the Jura mountains. His goodwill had been met with cynical treachery. Before he left Saint Domingue he spoke the following prophetic words:

> In overthrowing me, you have cut down in Saint Domingue only the trunk of the tree of liberty. It will spring up again by the roots for they are numerous and deep. (June 7, 1802)

On April 7, 1803, Toussaint L'Ouverture died in his prison cell, probably of pneumonia. But his example had taught the ex-slaves of Saint Domingue that they could defeat the world's greatest armies. Under the leadership of Jean-Jacques Dessalines, the war flared up again. Within a year, the French were defeated and Saint Domingue became the new, free state of Haiti. 'There's not a breathing of the common wind / That will forget thee', wrote William Wordsworth in a sonnet to the dead Toussaint: 'Thy friends are exultations, agonies, / And love, and Man's unconquerable mind.'

*In overthrowing me, you have cut down in Saint Domingue only the trunk of the tree of liberty. It will spring up again by the roots for they are numerous and deep.*

# ANTONIO MACEO

## 1845–1896

CUBA

Modern-day Cuba is proud of its historic links with Spain. In terms of its language, food and folk culture, it looks back to the hundreds of thousands of Spanish migrants who came to the island from the poverty-stricken regions of Estremadura or Galicia in search of a better life. Relations between the European nation and its former colony are usually cordial. Plane loads of Spanish tourists visit Cuba each week, many sympathetic to Fidel Castro's brand of socialism and hostility towards the United States (US).

But it was not much more than a century ago that Cuba and Spain were at war – a war ended by the military intervention of the US. It was a bitter conflict, the second of two Wars of Independence, and a turning-point in Spanish foreign policy. From it emerged a sort of independence for Cuba, although overshadowed by the US, and a number of legendary freedom fighters.

Remembered in Cuba as 'the Titan of Bronze', Antonio Maceo was a pivotal figure in the struggle for Cuban independence. He fought in both conflicts against the colonial power (1868–78 and 1895–98), but died in 1896 before he could see his dream of a free fatherland realised. He is held responsible for the extraordinary guerrilla campaign of 1895, in which Cuban rebels successfully took control of most of the island from a numerically superior Spanish army.

Antonio de la Caridad Maceo y Grajales was born in Santiago on June 14, 1845, the son of Marcos Maceo and Mariana Grajales, both opponents of Spanish rule. His father was white, his mother black, of Dominican origin. In 1868, a revolt broke out against the Spanish, led by Carlos Manuel de Céspedes, and Antonio, together with his father and three brothers joined the rebel army. Maceo rose swiftly through the ranks, leading many successful attacks on Spanish targets and developing a reputation as a fearless fighter. One contemporary described him on his gigantic horse, 'machete in hand, magnificent embodiment of the angel of destruction'.

The first War of Independence was losing its momentum in early 1878, as rebel leaders, unable to win a decisive military victory, were attracted by promises of reform and amnesty from the Spanish authorities. While the Dominican-born leader Máximo Gómez and others accepted the terms of the Pact of Zanjón, Maceo refused to lay down his arms, insisting that the fighting would not finish until Cuba had self-government and slavery was abolished. Known as the Baraguá Protest, Maceo's statement was a challenge both to the Spanish and to his less determined counterparts in the independence movement. Brave as his gesture was, however, Maceo could not carry on the fight alone and he went into exile.

Further attempts to rekindle the anti-Spanish rebellion failed, and for several years Maceo drifted from job to job in Jamaica and Honduras. In 1882, he was contacted by

José Martí, a leading pro-independence activist in New York, asking whether he would join forces in a fresh military uprising, but nothing more materialised for another decade. In 1886, Maceo moved to Panama, where he became involved in constructing housing for workers engaged on the Canal project. It was, by all accounts, a lucrative business, and his political activity temporarily faded, leaving Martí in New York to become the figurehead of the independence movement. After a brief return to Cuba in 1889, Maceo moved on to Costa Rica, where he established a farming colony on the Pacific coast at Nicoya. It seemed, for the time being at least, as though his commitment to Cuban freedom was weakening.

But by 1894, Maceo was once again in the forefront of the anti-Spanish movement. From Costa Rica he wrote hundreds of letters, seeking support and money from sympathisers. Now again in contact with Martí, he agreed to the plan for an island-wide insurrection in early 1895, intending to lead his own expedition from the eastern province of Oriente. Although frustrated by Martí's inability to provide him with the necessary resources, he set off from Costa Rica with 14 other fighters, arriving in Cuba in April. Escaping capture by Spanish forces, he quickly gathered insurgents around him, warning the population not to be deceived again by the empty promises that had been made in 1878.

It was at this point that Maceo met Martí to discuss the future shape of the struggle. Although attached to the same goal, there were fundamental differences between the two leaders. Martí, the white liberal, insisted that a civil organisation should control the military campaign; Maceo, the coloured military man, argued that a strong military command was needed until the Spanish were driven out. A few weeks later, Martí was dead.

After some successful encounters against the better-armed Spanish troops, Maceo and Máximo Gómez decided to cross the island from the eastern stronghold, to demonstrate that the rebels had support throughout the island. With great skill and audacity, Maceo led his men more than a thousand miles to the western province of Pinar del Rio, defeating Spanish troops along the way. Mostly armed with machetes, his army was, he admitted, inadequately equipped, but completely motivated:

> Our soldiers are not properly armed from any point of view . . . in spite of this, we have
> made great strides in our concept and we are constantly attaining improved conditions as
> we go into battle . . . Cuba should be free. The oppressed people have consecrated their
> lives to attain emancipation and God in heaven will strengthen their arms.
> (January 27, 1896)

Under the command of the repressive Valeriano Weyler, the Spanish began to fight back. In June, Maceo was badly wounded; the following month his brother, José, was killed. Herding villagers into concentration camps in an attempt to drain the rebellion of popular backing, Weyler began to surround Maceo in Pinar del Rio. In December 1896, Spanish troops attacked a farm where Maceo was resting. He was killed after a three-hour battle.

Maceo's death was greeted with jubilation in Spain and despair among supporters

*Our soldiers are not properly armed from any point of view ... in spite of this, we have made great strides in our concept and we are constantly attaining improved conditions as we go into battle ... Cuba should be free.*

of Cuban independence. But the military campaign appeared unstoppable. Máximo Gómez continued to inflict heavy defeats on the Spanish, and Weyler was eventually recalled to Spain. Then in 1898, what Martí and Maceo had both feared would happen took place. The US entered the conflict, signing a peace treaty with Spain at which no Cuban was present.

Maceo had warned that US intervention would spell the end of true independence. 'Liberty is conquered with the edge of a machete', he wrote, 'nor do I expect any benefit from the Americans.' In this, as in most matters of strategy and organisation, Maceo's instincts were right.

I n the struggle against slavery and oppression that followed the reverberations of the French Revolution names such as Toussaint L'Overture are justly celebrated. But there were many others who took up arms against slavery, and not all of them were black. The case of Louis Delgrès, the son of a white father and coloured mother, is one example of how the fight for liberation transcended racial categories and involved individuals of many differing backgrounds.

# LOUIS DELGRÈS

## 1766?–1802

GUADELOUPE

Louis Delgrès was born of mixed parentage into a wealthy and respectable family in the Martinican port city of Saint Pierre, probably in 1766. Martinique, like Guadeloupe, was at that time a French colony. The precise circumstances of his birth are not known, but it is thought that his mother, a Madame Guiby, was coloured and that he was therefore a free mulatto. In any case, we know that he joined the militia in 1783 and was promoted to sergeant in 1791. He had previously received a good education at his father's expense.

By now the French Revolution was in full flow, sweeping away much of the *ancien régime* and pittting France against the rest of Europe in a series of wars. Most importantly for the Caribbean, in 1794 the revolutionary Convention in Paris, a parliament dominated by radical Jacobins, voted to abolish slavery in the French colonies. A commissioner, Victor Hugues, was dispatched to Guadeloupe to implement the abolition, and rallying the liberated slaves to his side, he drove out a British force that had occupied the island earlier that year.

Meanwhile, Delgrès served with distinction in the Republican forces and was promoted to the rank of colonel at the age of 27. He fought against the British in Martinique in 1794 and was captured and then released. The following year he was instrumental in training the Antilles Battalion in the French port of Brest before returning to Guadeloupe. From there he fought against the British in St Lucia and St Vincent, where the French Republican forces supported the uprising of the Black Caribs.

Captured once more in 1796, Delgrès was shipped to Britain as prisoner-of-war before being freed in a prisoner exchange in 1797. Once again in France, he was promoted to *chef de bataillon* before setting sail to Guadeloupe in 1799. Now he was appointed aide-de-camp to the revolutionary agent Baco and then to his successor Lacrosse, nominated colonial prefect early in 1801.

By now, however, divisions, both political and personal, were creating tensions in Guadeloupe. Provoked by Lacrosse's authoritarian rule, a group of rebels decided to arrest and banish the prefect. Delgrès sided with the rebels, who enthusiastically welcomed him as a respected military leader. He was soon made a colonel and given the responsibility of commanding the garrison at Fort Saint Charles in Basse-Terre, the main town in the mountainous western part of the island.

There was a brief period of relative stability and prosperity, as the former slaves worked the land as peasant cultivators and conflict with Britain temporarily subsided. But this was not to last, as Napoleon Bonaparte, who had emerged triumphant from France's post-revolutionary struggles, was determined to reintroduce the system of slavery and return the French colonies to their old role as producers of wealth for the colonial elite. To this end, an expeditionary force, under the command of General Richepance, was sent to the Caribbean in April 1802, with the mission of reinstating slavery.

Delgrès, who had been described by his former superior as a *sans-culotte* (the most radical sort of Republican) was not prepared to countenance a return to the old order. When it became apparent that Richepance was indeed planning the reintroduction of slavery, Delgrès decided that he would fight against it. The French general was now the *de facto* ruler of Guadeloupe, and it was not long before he ordered the ex-slaves to be disarmed. Delgrès knew well that this was the first step in bringing back the tyranny of slavery. Richepance, for his part, considered Delgrès the most dangerous of potential rebels. As the French fleet sailed from Pointe-à-Pitre to Basse-Terre, Delgrès prepared his defences.

*A Louis Delgrès stamp*

An ultimatum came in the form of Richepance's order to Delgrès to surrender his command and disarm his garrison. Delgrès refused and instead rallied blacks and coloureds alike to his cause, handing out weapons. Pitted against him was a force of 700 battle-hardened Napoleonic troops, but Delgrès would not consider surrender. Instead, he issued a powerful appeal to the people of France:

> Even our former tyrants permitted a master to free his slaves. In this century of advanced thought and philosophy there still exist men who are so unjust and so powerful, and so far away, too, that they cannot think of black men except as slaves.

On May 12, 1802 an attack led by Delgrès' former ally, the mulatto Magloire Pélage, started a bloody siege of Fort Saint Charles. After heavy casualties on both sides, Delgrès decided to evacuate the fort and lead his men up into the hills of Matouba to the d'Anglemont Estate.

Richepance ordered his troops to mount an onslaught on Matouba. Delgrès, by now severely injured in the knee, withdrew into the Estate and decided that rather than surrender he would take his own life. Making a last stand, he famously said that he asked of posterity only remembrance and a tear for his brave men. As the French stormed the building, Delgrès deliberately kicked over a blazing charcoal stove, igniting the rebels' supply of gunpowder. A vast explosion killed Delgrès and his faithful followers as well as several French soldiers.

Delgrès' act of self-sacrifice was not enough to stop the reimposition of slavery and a further period of servitude until the final act of abolition in 1848. Yet his career, as well as his final heroic gesture, were evidence of a single-minded fight for freedom and justice. In Guadeloupe Fort Saint Charles was eventually renamed Fort Louis Delgrès in tribute to this man of integrity. In 2002, the 200th anniversary of his death, a fine sculpture of Delgrès' head was unveiled near the fort.

# INTO INDEPENDENCE

*Jean-Jacques Dessalines*

(Haiti)

*Juan Pablo Duarte*

(Dominican Republic)

*Norman Manley*

(Jamaica)

*Errol Barrow*

(Barbados)

Independence came relatively late to much of the Caribbean, but the quest for political freedom and the right to self-determination runs through much of the region's history. Colonisation, on the other hand, came early in comparison to Africa or Asia, and all of the Caribbean was effectively under European rule from the beginning of the seventeenth century. It took two centuries for the first, spectacular, process of independence to take place, the destruction of French Saint Domingue and the birth of Haiti. But the desire to throw off foreign domination began to manifest itself even before then, partly in the rebellions planned – and occasionally carried out – by slaves, and partly in the different sorts of resentment experienced by the European-descended colonists themselves. As early as 1650, for instance, the planters of Antigua and Barbados repudiated the Commonwealth government of Oliver Cromwell, proclaiming loyalty to Charles II. A fleet was dispatched to re-establish English rule over the mutinous colony.

Throughout the plantation period colonists and planters chafed against the monopolies demanded by the metropolitan countries. Spain, in particular, alienated those who lived and worked in its Caribbean colonies by extracting large taxes, insisting that the colonists trade only with Spanish merchants and sending over legions of incompetent and arrogant administrators. The resulting tension between *criollos* (Creoles or those of European ancestry born in the colony) and *peninsulares* (those arriving from Spain) was one of the root causes of the independence struggle throughout Latin America.

But Haiti's independence came first (second only in the Americas to that of the US) and unexpectedly. Saint Domingue was France's richest and most successful colony, the source of endless sugar, coffee and tobacco, a veritable cornucopia of tropical commodities. It was policed by a large and well-armed militia; the French navy was also one of the most efficient in the world at that time. Yet, within 13 years of the first slave uprising in 1791, not only France, but also Spain and Britain had been driven away from the colony by the sheer determination of its black population not to endure slavery or colonial domination any more. If Toussaint L'Ouverture had contemplated living in co-existence with the French, his successor, Jean-Jacques Dessalines, entertained no such illusions. His hatred of the French knew no bounds. It is said that he wished to write Haiti's declaration of independence and first constitution with the blood of a white man.

Ironically, the Caribbean's second successful move to independence involved not the overthrow of a European power, but the removal of Haitian forces from the neighbouring, formerly Spanish, part of Hispaniola. The birth of the Dominican Republic, under the idealistic leadership of Juan Pablo Duarte, was achieved only by the defeat of the region's first independent state. Even then, the road to real independence was a long and difficult one. In 1861, Dominican leaders actually invited Spain to re-colonise their country, hoping that this would deter further Haitian aggression. Four years later, Dominicans realised the extent of that misjudgment and again demanded self-rule.

The longest and most destructive independence struggle was that of Cuba against Spain, involving two full-scale wars (1868–78 and 1895–98) and the loss of thousands of lives. Had the US not intervened and finally expelled the Spanish from their last American colonies, it is difficult to know what the outcome would have been. But the US intervention effectively meant that Cuba did not win real independence, but rather a quasi-colonial status under the tutelage of Washington. It was American interference in Cuban politics, as predicted by Maceo and José Martí, that inspired a later generation of nationalists including one Fidel Castro.

Independence in the English-speaking Caribbean came without bloodshed or upheaval. In many senses, the British were happy to be relieved of their colonial obligations, and independence was arranged along constitutional lines. It was usually a gradual affair, with increasing self-government and greater popular participation from the 1940s onwards. But it required political leaders of vision and integrity, men such as Norman Manley and Errol Barrow, to steer their countries into full self-rule and nationhood. Some leaders fought for independence; others had it thrust upon them. But by the mid-1980s almost every former British colony was fully independent.

Today, a handful of territories remain attached to, or in part governed by, foreign powers. Martinique and Guadeloupe are technically parts of France, enjoying the same rights and constitutional guarantees as Normandy or Provence. The Dutch Antilles have also discovered a harmonious mode of cooperation with the authorities in The Hague. Perhaps least contented are the so-called 'overseas (formerly dependent) territories' of the UK – Anguilla, Montserrat, the British Virgin Islands, the Turks & Caicos islands and the Caymans – who often resent what they see as a lack of funding and the imposition of British legal bureaucracy. Yet none has demanded independence or even threatened to break away with any real conviction. They are too small, they insist, to go it alone.

Revered by many in Haiti as the architect of the country's independence, Dessalines enjoys an almost mythic status, greater even than that of Toussaint L'Ouverture. His cruelty and ruthlessness were legendary, as was his hatred of the white French colonialists of Saint Domingue, against whom he struggled during the 13-year war of independence. A fearless military leader and astute tactician, he was also a dictatorial ruler, inaugurating as the first leader of the independent country a long tradition of autocratic government in Haiti.

Jean-Jacques Dessalines was born in 1758, on the Cormiers plantation near the town of Grande-Rivière du Nord. He was at first owned by a brutal white plantation owner named Duclos, then sold to a free black master. In later years, it is said, Dessalines took pride in showing his whip-scarred back as a token of his hatred for slavery and the French. When the first revolt broke out among the slaves in 1791, Dessalines was quick to join the uprising, fighting on the side of Biassou, one of the main revolutionary leaders. By 1794, he had joined the forces of Toussaint L'Ouverture.

# JEAN-JACQUES DESSALINES
## 1758–1806
### HAITI

Dessalines first worked as a guide in the area of Grande-Rivière du Nord before rising to the rank of general. A loyal and trusted supporter of Toussaint, he was popular among the troops, refusing to adopt the French-influenced mannerisms of other leaders and showing pride in his African cultural heritage. It is recorded that he spoke an African dialect, as well as Creole, and that he practised *vodou*, the popular religion of the slaves. One eyewitness wrote that he was able to persuade his troops that to die in battle would mean an immediate return to the African homeland. As a result, his forces fought with what others saw as a fanatical disregard for their own lives.

By 1800, Dessalines, nicknamed 'the Tiger', had fought with distinction against the Spanish of Santo Domingo, a British expeditionary force that had hoped to snatch Saint Domingue from the French, and the mulatto forces of General André Rigaud. With his customary savagery, he took charge of reprisals against Rigaud's troops in the south of the island, giving orders for more than 300 officers to be shot. 'I said to prune the tree, not to uproot it,' commented Toussaint. But already, it seems, Dessalines had a very different view of Saint Domingue's future from Toussaint's. Whereas Toussaint envisaged some sort of compromise with the French and an eventual alliance with the paler-skinned mulatto population, Dessalines believed that only total independence and the triumph of the black majority would bring an end to the threat of slavery.

When Napoleon's huge military force arrived in December 1801, Dessalines realised that the French intended to reimpose their colonial rule and probably slavery too. Suspicious of the French promises of freedom, he at first followed Toussaint's order to

*I repeat, take courage, and you will see that when the French are few we shall harass them, we shall beat them, we shall burn the harvests and retire to the mountains. They will not be able to guard the country and they will have to leave. Then I shall make you independent. There will be no more whites among us.*

*Serge-Moléon-Blaise, Dessalines at Crête-à-Pierrot, 1981. Collection: Galerie Monnin*

cooperate with the occupying forces. But conflict soon broke out again and Dessalines was at the forefront of the fighting. The struggle for the strategically vital Crête-à-Pierrot fortress was one of the turning points of the war of independence. Although Dessalines was finally forced to abandon the fortress, he held it with 1,500 men against a French force ten times bigger. When eventually he broke through the surrounding French, his enemies had lost over 2,000 men. C.L.R. James describes how Dessalines during the siege, 'naked to the waist, with dirty boots, a hole in his hat where a bullet had passed through, patrolled the ramparts, glasses in hand.'

When Toussaint suddenly and unexpectedly made peace with the French, Dessalines at last began to see that his aim of winning complete independence would never be achieved while Toussaint was in charge. During the Crête-à-Pierrot siege, he had rallied his troops with the following words:

I repeat, take courage, and you will see that when the French are few we shall harass them, we shall beat them, we shall burn the harvests and retire to the mountains. They will not be able to guard the country and they will have to leave. Then I shall make you independent. There will be no more whites among us.

With Toussaint's arrest and deportation in June 1802, Dessalines's worst suspicions were justified. A brief stalemate followed, and then came the news that a French force had retaken the island of Guadeloupe and reimposed slavery there. The war began again in earnest, and Dessalines swiftly took command of the pro-independence army. As the French succumbed to yellow fever and guerrilla attacks, Dessalines made an alliance with Alexandre Pétion, the leader of the southern mulattoes. It was an unstoppable combination, assisted by a devastating epidemic of yellow fever among the French. Meeting French atrocities with atrocities of his own, Dessalines fought a merciless 'scorched earth' war. *Koupe tèt, boule kay* ('cut off their heads, burn down their houses') was his motto.

On April 7, 1803, Dessalines had symbolically ripped the white section from the French tricolore, thereby forming the flag of a new nation free from white oppression. On January 1, 1804, he was finally able to declare the independence of this nation, calling it Haiti after the indigenous Taino word *Ayiti* ('land of high mountains'). 'I have given the French cannibals blood for blood,' he declared, 'I have avenged America.'

The undisputed leader of the new country, Dessalines began his reign by removing the last traces of French influence. A series of bloody massacres took place in which nearly all surviving whites were killed. A new constitution was introduced, forbidding foreigners from owning property in Haiti and defining all Haitian citizens as 'black', irrespective of their real colour. Dessalines also began a radical land reform programme, seizing the former estates, many of them now owned by wealthy mulattoes, and handing out smallholdings to his ex-soldiers. His ambition was to restore the country's fortunes as a sugar and coffee exporter, but under the control of a strong government rather than foreigners.

As Dessalines grew more power-crazed and authoritarian, he declared himself emperor in October 1804. Ruling by fear, he persecuted the wealthier mulattoes, seeking to reward the thousands of ex-slaves who had fought with him. But eventually his enemies found the courage to plot against him and on October 17, 1806, Emperor Jean-Jacques I was ambushed and murdered near Port-au-Prince by a group of officers. His body was mutilated, but his legend grew still stronger. Dessalines's death, commemorated each year in Haiti, ushered in more than a century of political instability and gave birth to a durable myth of the resurrected liberator.

# JUAN PABLO DUARTE

### 1813–1876

DOMINICAN REPUBLIC

The modern-day Dominican Republic honours Duarte as 'the father of the nation', and his birthday on April 26 is a public holiday. With streets, neighbourhoods and even the counrty's highest mountain named after him, Duarte is remembered as the pioneer of Dominican independence and the idealistic leader who fought to end the Haitian occupation of his country. But Duarte's idealism was also perhaps his greatest flaw, as he was unable or unwilling to take part in the cynical political manoeuvering that followed independence, and was quickly sidelined.

Duarte was born in Santo Domingo, the son of a well-off ship's chandler, who had emigrated from Andalusia in 1795, and a locally-born mother. At that time Santo Domingo was the capital of the Spanish colony, occupying the western part of Hispaniola. But in 1822, the Haitian army, led by President Jean-Pierre Boyer, crossed the border from the eastern side and occupied the Spanish-speaking territory. Duarte's father was opposed to the Haitians, but the family remained in Santo Domingo. A clever boy at school, Juan Pablo was sent by his parents in 1828 to Europe to continue his studies. He visited London, Paris, Madrid and Barcelona, and the five-year stay in Europe seemed to have a profound effect on his thinking. Especially important was his witnessing of the 1830 July Revolution in France, where liberal and democratic forces rose up against a corrupt and repressive monarchy.

When Duarte returned to Santo Domingo in 1833, he was inspired by nationalist and liberal ideas and determined to end what he saw as the oppressive occupation of his country by the Haitians. Despite the enormous risks involved, he began to organise a secret society, known as La Trinitaria. Named partly after the holy Trinity and partly because the movement was divided into groups of three who each promised to enlist three more members, La Trinitaria worked slowly to build an underground resistance network. Gradually, more activists joined the movement, awaiting the moment when Boyer and his forces might be overthrown and a free country created in the former colony of Santo Domingo. The two other most prominent leaders were Ramón Mella and Francisco del Rosario Sánchez, and they in turn, with Duarte, gave another meaning to the word Trinitaria. In the years of cautious plotting Duarte even decided on a name for the future nation – La República Dominicana.

Duarte's long-awaited opportunity came in 1843, when Boyer began to face real opposition not just in Santo Domingo, but in Haiti. A disastrous earthquake the year before had created chaos, and various conspirators began to plan his downfall. Duarte and his colleagues allied themselves with one such dissident group led by Charles Hérard, which accused Boyer and his clique of corruption and dictatorial methods.

*I*t cannot be hoped that I (and with me any good Dominican) will stop protesting, and I will protest forever not only against the annexation of my country to the United States, but to any other power on the earth . . .

*La Trinitaria with Duarte seated in the centre.*

While Hérard led a revolt in Haiti, the Trinitarians easily ousted Boyer's main representatives in Santo Domingo. Within days Boyer was on a boat to Jamaica, bound for exile.

But if Duarte thought the next step to full independence would be as simple, he was mistaken. Hérard had no intention of giving up the western side of the island, and his troops began to crack down on those members of La Trinitaria who had identified themselves as pro-independence. Mella was arrested, Sánchez went into hiding, and Duarte escaped to Curaçao. At the same time, another anti-Haitian current was gathering strength in Santo Domingo, but this movement did not want independence as such, but separation from Haiti under French protection. This, its supporters believed, would prevent the Haitians from attempting to re-invade the country and guarantee its economic security. For several months, while Duarte waited anxiously in Curaçao, the various factions plotted and schemed.

Finally, on February 27, 1844, Mella gave the signal for the insurrection, and the Trinitarians seized important strategic locations in Santo Domingo and surrounded the Haitian garrison. The operation went smoothly and the following day a provisional junta received the Haitians' surrender and proclaimed the independence of the Dominican Republic. A ship was sent to fetch Duarte from Curaçao and he returned on March 14 to a hero's welcome and a seat in the governing junta.

The first priority was defending the new republic, as Hérard was planning an immediate re-invasion of the territory. Two forces of Haitian troops, numbering some 30,000 men, were dispatched that same month, and the Dominicans put up strong resistance both at Azua in the south and at Santiago further north. But even as the fighting was taking place, splits were appearing within the governing junta. A powerful figure, Pedro Santana, who had been instrumental in the anti-Haitian uprising, was now pressing for a deal by which the French would take over control of the territory. Together with other pro-annexationists, Santana realised that he would have to get rid of Duarte, who was resolutely opposed to any further foreign interference in his country. As the gulf between those who wanted a French protectorate and those who wanted independence widened, Santana accused Duarte, Mella and Sánchez of abusing their political power. All of them were condemned to exile in perpetuity in August 1844. Santana remained in power for the next two decades, finally inviting Spain to re-annex its former colony and return the Dominican Republic to colonial rule.

Duarte remained in exile in Venezuela for 20 years, watching events in his homeland with dismay. He returned briefly in 1864 as the Dominicans were again engaged in a war of independence, this time against Spain, and saw Mella on his deathbed. But by now Duarte was an irrelevance in the real world of Dominican politics and he accepted a minor post as diplomatic agent in Venezuela, where he died in poverty in 1876.

Only later did Duarte become a national hero, symbolising the values of patriotism and self-sacrifice. In a letter written to the Dominican Foreign Minister in 1864, he expressed these values:

> It cannot be hoped that I (and with me any good Dominican) will stop protesting, and I will protest forever not only against the annexation of my country to the United States, but to any other power on the earth, and at the same time against any treaty that seeks in whatever way to damage our national independence or any of the rights of the Dominican people.

# NORMAN MANLEY

## 1893–1969

JAMAICA

Of the many accomplished men and women who were instrumental in leading the English-speaking Caribbean towards independence in the 1960s and 1970s, Norman Manley stands out as one of the most gifted. A talented sportsman, lawyer and scholar, he was also a passionate political activist who stood up for the most disadvantaged sectors of Jamaica's population and who believed deeply in the cause of a united Caribbean. He might have succeeded equally as an athlete or barrister, but it was in the fight for Jamaican independence and in the creation of its first real political party that he left his mark.

Norman Washington Manley was born at Roxborough, near Mandeville in the parish of Manchester, of mixed Irish and African ancestry and was light-skinned. The family moved when he was six years old, his father having died, to Guanaboa Vale in Clarendon, and it was there that his older cousin, Alexander Clarke (later to be known as Alexander Bustamante) came to live with them. In later life, Norman Manley and Bustamante were to be first political associates and then, for many years, adversaries. Manley was a gifted student and did well at St Jago, Wolmers' and finally Jamaica College. But what he really excelled at was athletics, and in his teens he was a record-breaking sprinter and hurdler. If it had not been for the outbreak of the First World War, it is possible that he might have won medals at Olympic level.

When war broke out, Manley was already in England, having won a Rhodes Scholarship to study law at Oxford University. He and his brother Roy both enlisted in the British army, and Norman was promoted to the rank of corporal in the royal artillery. Tragically, Roy was killed in action in the trenches of Flanders (Norman wore a black tie in his brother's memory for the rest of his life). When the war ended, he continued his studies and qualified as a lawyer, representing several West Indians in law cases in England. He also married his first cousin, Edna Swithenbank, an artist and later to be a celebrated sculptress.

Manley returned to Jamaica in 1922, quickly establishing himself as a formidable defence lawyer who reputedly never lost a murder case he defended. For the next 15 years his reputation grew in legal circles, but he also became increasingly interested in politics and social issues. His work brought him into daily conflict with the victims of social injustice and poverty in colonial Jamaica, and he began to believe that the future of Jamaica would be more secure in Jamaican hands. The wave of social unrest that swept through the Caribbean in the late 1930s reinforced these beliefs, especially when a strike at the Frome sugar factory in Westmoreland led to serious violence and several deaths. At the centre of the disturbances was Manley's cousin, Bustamante, having returned from nearly 30 years of travels around the world and now a rabble-

*I say that the mission of my generation was to win self-government for Jamaica. To win political power which is the final power for the black masses of my country from which I spring. I am proud to stand here today and to say to you who fought that fight with me . . .*

Norman Manley addressing a group on the docks.

rousing trade union organiser. When 'Busta' was thrown into jail by the colonial authorities, Manley intervened and secured his release.

By now, Manley's ambitions were increasingly political, and having founded an organisation called Jamaica Welfare to help poor rural communities, he decided to throw himself into party politics. In 1938, he and a group of like-minded Jamaicans formed the People's National Party (PNP), pledged to achieve universal adult suffrage and a much greater degree of self-government. For a time he was joined by Bustamante, but in 1943 the latter broke away from the PNP and formed his own Jamaica Labour Party. The political differences between the two cousins ran deep; while Manley believed in a moderate brand of socialism and argued for much greater cooperation between Caribbean territories, the more pragmatic Bustamante, despite being a trade union leader, saw private enterprise as the solution to Jamaica's problems and was much less interested in regional politics. It was Bustamante who capitalised on the first election held under universal suffrage in 1944 with his populist promises of better wages and conditions, and Manley had to wait until 1955 for the PNP to win a general election.

By then Manley was convinced that Jamaican independence could best be achieved within the wider context of a federal structure, bringing together the English-speaking Caribbean territories into a single independent state. As early as 1945, Manley had argued that 'it is impossible to assume that each island, even the largest, could by itself be in a position to provide the basic necessities of a modern state.' Encouraged by the British, who did not wish their colonies to become independent as tiny individual territories, the federal plan gathered impetus, and after a series of meetings, elections were held in all ten islands for a federal government to sit in Port of Spain, Trinidad.

At this point, Manley made the first of two political mistakes. He refused the leadership of the Federation, thereby allowing Grantley Adams of Barbados, a less able politician, to become prime minister. Manley was perhaps more concerned with maintaining his position as Chief Minister of Jamaica and realised that the anti-Federation Bustamante would have greater influence if he was often absent in Trinidad. He also feared that without his presence, the PNP might split into warring factions. Gradually, moreover, the Federation began to show signs of strain, as Jamaica and Trinidad, the two 'big powers', argued over economic matters. Bustamante seized on hostility to the Federation in Jamaica and demanded a referendum to allow Jamaicans to vote on its future. True to his democratic principles, Manley agreed, hence making his second mistake. The vote was duly in favour of Jamaica leaving the Federation, and Manley not only saw his ideal collapse, but was widely blamed for its failure.

In the aftermath of the federal experiment, Manley moved quickly to assure Jamaica's independence from Britain. Ironically, however, it was Bustamante's JLP that won elections in early 1962, buoyed by its successful campaign against the Federation. After all his hard work, Manley had to witness the advent of independence as leader of the opposition, a position he held until shortly before his death.

In his last speech to a PNP conference, Manley looked back on his achievements:

> I say that the mission of my generation was to win self-government for Jamaica. To win political power which is the final power for the black masses of my country from which I spring. I am proud to stand here today and to say to you who fought that fight with me, say it with gladness and pride, 'Mission accomplished for my generation' . . . And what is this the mission of this generation? It is reconstructing the social and economic life of Jamaica.

Present at the conference was Norman Manley's son, Michael, who took over the leadership of the PNP in September 1969. Within three years he was prime minister of Jamaica, following his father's commitment to social reform and democratic politics.

# ERROL BARROW
## 1920–1987
BARBADOS

Barbados's enviable modern record as one of the developing world's most successful societies owes much to the work of Errol Barrow, the man who led the island to independence and presided over a long period of stability. It has been said of Barrow that he found in Barbados 'a collection of villages and transformed them into a proud nation.' He also took the side of the poorer members of that nation against the traditional vested interests of large landowners, introducing reforms that changed the lives of many Barbadians for the better.

Errol Walton Barrow was born on January 21, 1920 into a family of social reformers. His father, an Anglican priest, had been removed from his pulpit in St Croix after local conservatives complained that the sermons he delivered to his poor congregation were too progressive. His uncle, Dr Charles Duncan O'Neale, was a doctor who was involved in the first radical trade union movement in Barbados. His older sister, Nita, would become an international activist against apartheid and Barbados's representative at the United Nations after a distinguished career in public health and adult education.

The 1930s were a period of great social unrest in the Caribbean, and Barbados was no exception. The young Errol Barrow lived through and witnessed the disturbances of the period, especially the rioting and deaths that followed the deportation of the union activist Clement Payne in 1937. He realised from an early age that economic injustice and political exclusion lay behind the riots in Barbados and from his parents he gained an understanding of the huge obstacles facing the poor majority.

In 1940, Barrow went to England, where he joined the Royal Air Force (RAF) during the critical Battle of Britain. He served in the RAF throughout the Second World War and then remained in London, where he studied law and economics. He returned to Barbados in 1950 as a qualified barrister, and the following year joined the Barbados Labour Party (BLP), which had been founded by Grantley Adams in 1938. That same year, an election took place – the first to be held under a system of universal adult suffrage – and Barrow was elected to the Barbados House of Assembly as a BLP member for the parish of St George.

At the time, colonial Barbados was still dominated, politically and economically, by a small, mostly white, class of landowners and businessmen, sometimes known as the 'plantocracy'. Since the first British settlement of Barbados, this minority of wealthy businessmen and farmers had wielded disproportionate influence in Barbadian society. Grantley Adams was aware of this group's power and adopted a cautious approach towards dismantling their privileges. For Barrow and other more radical BLP members, Adams's conservative tactics proved the source of great frustration, especially as the BLP enjoyed a large majority and extensive public support. Barrow and others believed that the BLP could move much more quickly and effectively against the plantocracy – for the benefit of the majority, mostly poor, population.

By 1954, Barrow had lost patience with the BLP's conservative approach, especially in the face of mounting unemployment and widespread hardship throughout Barbados. In a famous speech in the House of Assembly he criticised the BLP and announced that he was leaving Adams's party:

> I am going to make serious statement now because I regard this [unemployment] as the most pressing problem facing this island at present, and in view of the fact that I am completely dissatisfied not only with the Honourable Minister of Labour, but with the whole attitude of ministers of the Government and their complete disregard of the suffering of the people . . . Because of that, I no longer want to be associated with them politically or otherwise . . .

With a number of followers and supporters, Barrow then established his own rival political organisation, the Democratic Labour Party (DLP) in April 1955. It already had several members in the House of Assembly and strong support among trade unionists, but the new party faced an uphill struggle in wooing voters away from the BLP. In the 1956 general election, it won four seats against the BLP's 15 and Barrow failed to be re-elected in his St George seat. But the setback was temporary; two years later, a by-election in St John enabled Barrow to re-enter the House.

Over the next three years Barrow's popularity gradually rose as Adams's fell. The brief and unsuccessful Federation of the West Indies was enthusiastically supported by Adams, and when the experiment collapsed, his name and reputation were tarnished. Another damaging factor was the 1958 sugar crisis, in which the BLP had appeared anti-worker in its reluctance to improve wages. Barrow was able to capitalise on the government's growing unpopularity, presenting himself as the radical alternative to Adams. The DLP entered the 1961 general elections with the optimistic manifesto slogan 'operation takeover' and with a groundswell of support from working Barbadians and young voters. The election was a triumph for Barrow: 16 DLP members versus only five for the BLP. At the age of 41, Errol Barrow became Premier of Barbados.

For the next five years the government enacted a sweeping series of reforms aimed at modernising the island's economy and society. Free secondary education for all was introduced along with a national insurance scheme. The health system, from rural clinics to hospitals, was built up, while workers were guaranteed higher wages and expanded rights at work. Barrow's government also wanted to improve Barbados's economy and to reduce its dependence on old-fashioned sugarcane production. Foreign companies were encouraged to open factories on the island and tourism became a major employer as the government supported hotel construction and international marketing.

Such was the government's popularity that Britain welcomed Barrow's demand for independence – a goal to which he had long aspired. On November 30, 1966, Barbados

*A moderate nationalist and political reformer, Barrow is honoured each year on January 21 by the people of Barbados. He will long be remembered as one of the main architects of the Barbadian success story.*

*Barrow hoisted by a group of supporters.*

followed Jamaica, Trinidad and British Guiana into full independence, with Errol Barrow as the country's first prime minister. It was perhaps the greatest achievement of his career.

Over the next decade, Barrow remained in power, guiding the island's development with a moderate but fundamentally progressive brand of politics. Barbados escaped the political tribulations of the period and earned a reputation for stability and modest prosperity. Only in 1976 was the BLP, under the leadership of John 'Tom' Adams, Grantley's son, able to stage a comeback. Errol Barrow went into opposition for ten years.

In 1986 Barrow was back, as the DLP won another landslide victory. But tragically he was to serve only just over a year as prime minister before his sudden and unexpected death. The mourning in Barbados was deep and genuine, for Barrow was seen by many as a sort of father figure and as a man of real integrity. Far from being aloof, he enjoyed a reputation as approachable and fun-loving. He even co-authored a cookery book, entitled *Privilege,* a celebration of Caribbean cooking and its varied cultural roots.

A moderate nationalist and political reformer, Barrow is honoured each year on January 21 by the people of Barbados. He will long be remembered as one of the main architects of the Barbadian success story.

# POLITICS AND POWER

*Luis Muñoz Marín*

(Puerto Rico)

*Sir Alexander Bustamante*

(Jamaica)

*Aimé Cesairé*

(Martinique)

*Fidel Castro*

(Cuba)

*Lucette Michaux-Chevry*

(Guadeloupe)

P olitics are as important in the Caribbean as anywhere else in the world. At times they are the subject of gossip, a target for fun. At others, they can amount to an obsession and even lead to violence. Each island has its own political peculiarities, its own specific rivalries and traditions. In some places, such as Jamaica, political parties are well established, with a network of branches and activists. Elsewhere, as in Haiti, parties have always been less significant than personalities, who have tended to use them as vehicles for their own ambitions. But everywhere elections bring out the best and worst in people: humour and hatred, debate and prejudice, idealism and cynicism.

The political landscape of the Caribbean has been mixed since the 1950s. Cuba, of course, stands out as one of the last bastions of communism in a globalised capitalist world. Until recently, Haiti was a byword for dictatorship and repression, and remains volatile. After decades of autocratic rule, the Dominican Republic is today a functioning democracy, with keenly fought elections. Across the English-speaking Caribbean, multi-party systems and parliamentary procedure are the norm.

But in many cases, this stability is of recent origins. Indeed, the shape of particular political systems in the Caribbean is generally a product of events in the latter part of the twentieth century. In that sense, politics as we know them in the region are a relatively modern invention. The Cuban Revolution was one determining factor, as was the overthrow of dictatorships in Haiti and the Dominican Republic. Independence also changed the political landscape from the 1960s onwards. But there were also other significant events, and there were also a handful of individual personalities who shaped the future course of their own countries.

Puerto Rico's relationship with the US has come under intense scrutiny and criticism since the elaboration of the 'free associated state' arrangement in 1952. Yet the architect of this relationship, Luis Muñoz Marín, is generally regarded as a key figure in Puerto Rico's dramatic transformation from a neglected backwater to a modern, developed economy. Some Puerto Ricans may yearn for independence (and more for full incorporation into the US), but not enough for Muñoz Marín's constitutional formula to have been changed in the last half century.

Another politician who inspired the enmity of his pro-independence opponents is Aimé Césaire, whose vision of an autonomous Martinique within the French Republic survives to this day. Critics have accused Césaire of perpetuating colonialism, but the great majority of Martinicans are satisfied with their relationship with *la patrie*. Césaire was not only a formidable politician during his long career, but also a significant poet, whose masterpiece, *Return to My Native Land*, has been judged to be one of the twentieth century's literary landmarks.

Independence in the English-speaking Caribbean also produced a generation of memorable and exceptional political leaders. In Jamaica, the flamboyant Alexander Bustamante rose to prominence through the turmoil of the 1930s and was able to create one of the island's two enduring political parties as well as its first powerful trade union. Opposed to his cousin, Norman Manley, Bustamante represented the populist tradition of the charismatic leader that runs through the Caribbean's politics. Others in that mould included the controversial figures of Eric Gairy (Grenada), Robert Bradshaw (St Kitts-Nevis) and Vere Bird (Antigua-Barbuda). Another controversial politician – and a very visible exception as a woman – was Dame Eugenia Charles, who was prime minister of Dominica from 1980 to 1995. She is probably best remembered for her role in the October 1983 crisis in Grenada, when she publicly welcomed the US intervention after the murder of Maurice Bishop.

The pursuit of political power has marked the recent history of those troubled neighbours, Haiti and the Dominican Republic. Joaquín Balaguer, once the puppet president of the dictator Rafael Leonidas Trujillo, stood in no fewer than ten times for the presidency, enjoying seven terms in office, before retiring at the age of 94. The Duvalier dynasty in Haiti showed a similar stubborn attachment to power, 'Papa Doc' ruling from 1957 until 1971 and his son 'Baby Doc' taking over until 1986. Since then, a succession of coups and disputed elections have frustrated the Haitian people's desire for democracy.

If all the above have at one time or another wielded considerable power, none can compete with Fidel Castro, the longest surviving political leader in the world. Probably one of the few politicians to be a household name around the world, Castro has dominated Cuba – and the Caribbean political scene – for four decades. American presidents come and go, but Castro has outlived them all. His career is a testimony to the art of political survival and an example of the difficulty of relinquishing absolute power.

Today's Puerto Rico has all the trappings of US-style modernity. Skyscrapers loom over the financial district of the capital, San Juan, while luxury hotels and condominiums stretch along the coastline. Busy highways link comfortable-looking suburbs to shopping malls and drive-in fast food outlets; huge billboards vaunt the virtues of American cars, credit card companies and internet services. Remote mountainside villages may still retain their rural tranquillity, but the urban sprawl throbs to the pulse of rampant consumerism.

Puerto Rico's prosperity is a recent development. In the 1940s, the island was among the poorest and most desperate corners of the Caribbean, topping statistical tables for poverty, illness and deprivation. After centuries of colonial neglect from Spain and four decades of incompetent rule from the US, it was on the verge of a social explosion. Nationalists demanding independence from the US had resorted to terrorist tactics; some US politicians were in favour of cutting Puerto Rico adrift.

The transition from tropical slum to modern-day 'developed' status was in large part the work of Luis Muñoz Marín, a politician who combined day-to-day pragmatism with a clear vision of how he wanted his homeland to develop. He believed that Puerto Rico's future lay not in independence (he had viewed the woes of independent Haiti and the Dominican Republic with concern), but in a close and yet non-colonial relationship with the US. This belief earned him many enemies among those who wanted Puerto Rico to break away from American control, but it also brought about a spectacular transformation in the island's identity.

# LUIS MUÑOZ MARÍN

## 1898–1980

### PUERTO RICO

Muñoz Marín was born in San Juan in 1898, the year that US forces took control of the island during the Spanish-American War. His father was a well-known journalist and politician, and his childhood was divided between Puerto Rico and the US as his father worked and campaigned in San Juan and New York. He did not complete his law studies at Georgetown University and instead returned in 1916 to Puerto Rico with his ailing father, who died that year.

The young Muñoz Marín wanted, above all, to be a poet, and for the next few years he made a precarious living by writing poetry, literary criticism and articles for a number of newspapers and journals, mostly in the US. He was more often than not in New York, and it was there that he became involved in politics, joining the Socialist Party in 1920.

After more than a decade in the US, Muñoz Marín returned to Puerto Rico in 1931, determined to make a contribution in politics. At that time, the island was suffering the consequences of the Great Depression, and unemployment and malnutrition had reached epidemic proportions. He at first joined the Liberal Party, taking over the

*... People of Puerto Rico trust that they will be able to live happily and calmly according to their traditional understanding and attitudes ...*

*Puerto Rico: Muñoz Marín* (right) *congratulates Sánchez Vilella, his successor, on his victory, November, 1964.*

editorship of its newspaper *La Democracia*, and was then elected as a senator in 1932. In 1937, however, he was expelled from the party, accused of mishandling its unsuccessful election campaign the previous year. In 1938, Muñoz Marín formed his own organisation, the Popular Democratic Party, pledged to stamp out the corruption and conservatism of the existing parties.

For the next two years, Muñoz Marín travelled the length and breadth of the island, holding political meetings and explaining to rural voters that they should no longer sell their votes to the old parties for two dollars each. Instead, he inspired his growing number of supporters with the message that life could be improved in Puerto Rico through honest government and a proper series of social reforms. The result of the 1940 election was a complete surprise: Muñoz Marín's party won enough seats for him to become President of the Senate and to implement his reform programme. This involved land reform (companies were forbidden to have landholdings over 500 acres), the state control of much of the sugar industry, trade union rights and long overdue infrastructural development. The appointment of a progressive US governor, Rexford G Tugwell, contributed enormously to the success of Muñoz Marín's reforms.

In 1947, the US Congress approved a move to allow Puerto Ricans to elect their own governor. The following year, Muñoz Marín was elected with a huge majority. For the next 16 years he presided over three main areas of reform, each of which he dubbed an 'operation'. The first, *Opereracíon Manos a la Obra* (Operation Bootstrap) was intended to bring increased employment and prosperity to the island by rapid industrialisation. The key was foreign investment, and Muñoz Marín enacted laws giving tax breaks and subsidies to companies, mostly from the US, which opened up factories on the island. Attracted by low taxes and cheap labour rates, over 100 factories opened between 1947 and 1950, mostly assembling garments and electrical components. His critics argued that they were exploiting Puerto Rican workers, but Muñoz Marín pointed to falling unemployment and rising average income. The foreign businesses continued to arrive over the following years, and many are still there, especially in the pharmaceutical and chemical sectors.

Muñoz Marín's second 'operation' involved Puerto Rico's constitutional status. Rejecting the two old alternatives (independence or full incorporation into the US), he put in motion the election of a constituent assembly and the drafting of a new constitution, to be approved by popular referendum. After much discussion, the formula reached by the constituent assembly was that of a 'free associated state' of the US. This formula was approved by a popular vote in 1952. This meant that Puerto Ricans enjoyed a large degree of self-government, remained US citizens, but were not entitled to vote in US national elections. This system, also known as commonwealth status, has remained in force to this day, despite strong opposition from proponents of independence and full statehood.

The final operation was *Operación Serenidad* (Serenity), in which Muñoz Marín sought to develop education and cultural achievement in the island. The plan, he said:

> strives to add to economic strength and political freedom some objectives in harmony with the spirit of man, in his role as governor rather than servant of economic processes . . . the people of Puerto Rico trust that they will be able to live happily and calmly according to their traditional understanding and attitudes, while having full and vigorous access to all the complex resources of modern civilisation.

By this Muñoz Marín envisaged literacy classes, the promotion of local art and cinema and the creation of the prestigious Conservatory of Music, to which he invited the world famous cellist Pablo Casals as director.

After 16 years of intense political work, Muñoz Marín retired from the governorship in 1964, although he remained a senator and led his Popular Democratic Party in the 1968 elections. He finally retired in 1970 and lived another ten years in San Juan, devoting much time to advising on US-Puerto Rican relations. His death was the occasion of a huge funeral cortege that took 12 hours to reach the village of Barranquitas where he was buried.

Today Muñoz Marín is remembered by most Puerto Ricans with great respect, although some believe that he was responsible for tying the island into a humiliating dependency on the US. Even his strongest critics, however, cannot deny that his policies were effective in reducing the chronic poverty of the 1940s, even at the expense of national sovereignty.

# SIR ALEXANDER BUSTAMANTE
## 1884–1977
### JAMAICA

A trade union leader, politician and National Hero, Bustamante played a vital part in Jamaica's transition from a British colony to an independent nation. His concern for the welfare of poor Jamaicans and his ability to communicate with them, won him a massive following and enabled him to establish one of Jamaica's main political parties. Although conservative in many of his attitudes, he achieved radical improvements for many workers and ensured the peaceful development of the independence process.

Bustamante was born William Alexander Clarke on February 24, 1884, changing his name later. His childhood home was at Blenheim, in the parish of Hanover, and his father was an Irishman, his mother a pale-skinned Jamaican of part-Indian descent. He was also a cousin of Norman Manley, with whom he was later to collaborate and then contest in the field of politics. By all accounts, he was not a particularly academic child, but was known as a good horseman, able to tame local farmers' wild horses. At the age of 20 he worked for a year at the Manley home at Belmont in the parish of Clarendon. The next year, in 1905, he set off on a long series of travels that took him to Spain, Cuba, Panama and the US.

For 27 years Bustamante moved around the world, at one point joining the Spanish army and adopting the name Bustamante from a Spanish sea captain who had befriended him. He later worked in the US and made a significant sum of money from dealing on the Stock Exchange in New York. When he finally returned to Jamaica in 1932, Bustamante was a man of wide experience, ready to involve himself in the political life of his island. Jamaica at the time was in the grip of the world-wide Depression, with sugar prices at rock bottom and unemployment rife. Although a man of substance and a money-lender by profession, Bustamante was appalled at the deprivation suffered by rural sugar workers and the unemployed poor in Kingston and other towns. Writing to newspapers and prominent public figures, he warned that Jamaica was facing a social crisis:

> The pot of discontent is boiling, today it has reached the brim, tomorrow it may overflow.

In May 1938, Bustamante's prediction became reality, as sugar workers went on strike, followed by dockers and council workers in Kingston. The strikes turned into riots and clashes with the police, in which eight people were killed, nearly 200 wounded and 700 arrested. Bustamante, who had previously joined and left the Jamaica Workers' and Tradesmen's Unions, saw the disturbances as an opportunity to build a strong workers' movement in Jamaica. Tirelessly addressing meetings at plantations and on the streets of Kingston, he urged the strikers to stand up for their

*Alexander Bustamante in a characteristic pose, speaking during the 1938 Riots.*

rights and to join together in a strong trade union. His skill at addressing the crowds in direct language that they understood, won him a large following, and this was reinforced by the courage he showed in dealing with the authorities. At one meeting, the police threatened to open fire and Bustamante reportedly opened his shirt and invited them to shoot him instead of the strikers. He also openly called for the colonial Governor to be removed. On May 24, he was thrown into jail.

The disturbances quickly died down, but 'Busta' had become a popular hero. After Norman Manley, by now an eminent barrister, had secured his release from prison, Bustamante threw himself into building a trade union movement that he baptised the Bustamante Industrial Trade Union (BITU). He also joined Manley's People's National Party (PNP), working for a while alongside his cousin. But Bustamante and Manley already had different views of how to bring about change in Jamaica, and Bustamante was convinced that trade union activity was the best way forward. In 1939, dock workers went on strike, and he encouraged other workers to join in a General Strike. He was arrested by the colonial authorities in 1942, charged with sedition and jailed for 17 months.

Finally released in 1943, Bustamante decided to break away from Manley, whose moderate socialist views he did not share, and to form his own party, the Jamaica Labour Party (JLP). Strongly linked to the BITU, this organisation campaigned for higher wages and better working conditions in the first ever elections held with full adult suffrage in 1944. With its slogan 'Bread and Butter', the JLP promised immediate social reforms rather than talking about independence and it won again in 1949. Bustamante remained Chief Minister for 11 years. In 1954 he was knighted by Queen Elizabeth II.

Voted out in 1955 and losing again in 1959, the JLP took a critical stance towards the planned West Indies Federation, which was enthusiastically supported by Manley and the PNP. Warning that Jamaica would have to subsidise the poorer, smaller islands in the federal structure, Bustamante demanded that Jamaica should withdraw altogether from the Federation and forced Manley into holding a referendum on the subject. A majority of Jamaicans voted in favour of withdrawal, leading to the collapse of the Federation and speeding the movement towards Jamaican independence. Many blamed Bustamante for wrecking the federation, but he was unrepentant, arguing that Jamaica would lose its sovereignty in a multi-island federal administration.

As the agreed date for independence approached, elections were held and the JLP won a resounding victory. As a result, Bustamante became the independent country's first prime minister on August 5, 1962. The smooth transition from colony to nationhood was largely credited to him.

In the five years that followed, Bustamante introduced some long overdue reforms in the ownership of land and a carefully thought through Five-Year Development Plan. He also aligned the island firmly on the side of the US, turning his back on Fidel Castro's revolution in Cuba and declaring at the United Nations, 'I am for the West. I am against Communism.' In his later years, Bustamante showed little of the radicalism of the 1930s, but he remained a charismatic personality and an excellent orator, unmistakable through his shock of unruly white hair. Retiring from politics in 1967, he lived quietly until his death on August 6, 1977.

Although Bustamante was very much less educated than his cousin and political adversary Norman Manley, his influence on Jamaican politics was enormous. His populist style and skill in rough-and-tumble politics earned him a solid following, while his commitment to democratic means safeguarded Jamaica's constitutional system during some of the island's most turbulent moments.

*Although Bustamante was very much less educated than his cousin and political adversary Norman Manley, his influence on Jamaican politics was enormous.*

*Norman Manley* (left) *then Premier, shares a joke with Sir Alexander Bustamante after the formal signing of the Independence Conference Report, Lancaster House, February 1962.*

Visitors to Martinique are often amazed at how French the island appears. From the boulangeries and képi-wearing policemen to the traffic jams full of Renault cars, the island can look like a tropical outpost of France – which is what it is. The close relationship between Martinique and its former colonial ruler is based on nearly 500 years of history, but its actual form is very much the work of one man.

Aimé Césaire dominated both politics and literature in Martinique for almost half a century. An astute politician, convinced of the validity of his vision for the ex-colony, he inspired great loyalty and fierce criticism. He will be remembered both for his role in turning Martinique into a full-fledged department of France and, paradoxically, for his poetic outbursts against 'Western' civilisation.

Aimé Fernand Césaire was born on June 26, 1913 at Basse-Pointe, a small town on Martinique's north coast. His family was part of the island's small black middle class, with his father employed as a tax inspector. The family moved to Fort-de-France, where Césaire attended the Lycée Schoelcher and in 1931 he won a scholarship to study in Paris. There he met and worked with a group of black students and intellectuals from both Francophone Africa and the Caribbean, contributing his writing to various radical journals.

# AIMÉ CÉSAIRE

1913 –

MARTINIQUE

Césaire is normally credited with coining the term *négritude*, which became an influential literary and philosophical set of ideas in the 1930s. Rejecting the dominance of Western rationalism, with its view of Europe as the centre of civilisation, *négritude* argued that Africa and the African diaspora had their own authentic cultural values, which white racism had always denigrated.

In 1939, Césaire returned to Martinique, where he taught at the Lycée Schoelcher, inspiring a generation of students which included the revolutionary psychiatrist Frantz Fanon. He had also had a first version of his poem 'Cahier d'un retour au pays natal' published in a Parisian journal, *Volontés*, but the poem had passed unnoticed.

The war years were particularly harsh for Martinique whose white colonial rulers had sided with Pétain's Vichy regime and which was blockaded by the US navy in 1942–43. The enforced presence of thousands of French sailors encircled by a US fleet, doubtless reinforced Césaire's hatred of racism. The emergence of the French Communist Party (PCF) as the leading anti-Vichy force was another important development and by 1942, he was a member. After a lecture tour in Haiti in 1944, Césaire returned to a Martinique in political turmoil, where the PCF was capitalising on long pent-up aspirations for change in the colonial system. In 1945, Césaire was elected mayor of Fort-de-France and *député* to the French parliament, both on a PCF ticket.

With the French colonies stagnating after decades of neglect and the privations of the war, Césaire and his colleagues on the Left, both in Paris and the Caribbean,

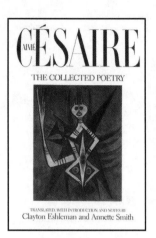

*Berkeley: University of California Press, 1994.*

favoured political integration over independence, arguing that a 'rational dependence' on France would quickly raise living standards through massive subsidies. The PCF-sponsored legislation creating the *union française* was supported in a 1946 referendum and Martinique and the other colonies became *départements d'outre mer* (DOMs) or overseas departments of France, theoretically on a constitutional par with any French *département*. This meant that Martinicans (as well as Guadeloupeans and French Guyanese) were full and equal citizens of France.

But the rapid improvements anticipated by Césaire were slow to materialise. A highly centralised system of government from Paris gave too much power to a Prefect; the subsidies from France were inadequate to rebuild the run-down island infrastructure. In 1958, Césaire voted in support of Charles de Gaulle's constitutional reforms, which created the Fifth Republic and replaced the union with the *communauté française*. These gave more political autonomy to the DOMs and also allowed Césaire to elaborate a political position which he held more or less consistently for the rest of his career: increased autonomy within a departmental relationship with France. In 1958 he also formed the Progressive Martinican Party (PPM), an organisation which supported departmentalisation but demanded greater freedoms from metropolitan control.

Re-elected mayor of Fort-de-France at every subsequent election and a *député* until his retirement in 1995, Césaire was an efficient administrator and the personification of a status quo that most Martinicans found acceptable. As a result of his strategy, they have enjoyed above-average incomes and social services, funded by subsidies from France.

*Césaire's Cahier d'un retour au pays natal* (1939), translated as *Return to My Native Land*, has been described by critic Roberto Márquez as 'perhaps the single most celebrated, sustained, and representatively compendious lyrical monument to *négritude*.' According to legend, a roneoed copy of the poem was discovered in 1942 by André Breton, the eminent surrealist poet, in a haberdasher's shop in Fort-de-France. Breton was responsible for its republication in Paris after the war, and the poem became the standard text of *négritude*. In a series of discordant, and often discomforting images, Césaire spurns the French colonial concept of assimilation ('Accommodate yourself to me/I won't accommodate myself to you') before tracing the route back from Martinique to Africa, the origin of the slaves whose descendants make up the majority of Martinicans. The poem's tone is both apocalyptic and lyrical as it demands the end of Eurocentric arrogance and the beginning of a new black solidarity:

> No race holds a monopoly of beauty, intelligence and strength
> there is room for all at the meeting-place of conquest

The apparent contradiction between the poetic radicalism and the political pragmatism did not escape Césaire's later critics, many of whom blame him for having extended French control over Martinique and lost the opportunity for independence. Even so, few deny him a significant place in the history of twentieth-century poetry and Caribbean literature.

Few Cubans can remember a world without Fidel Castro. For more than four decades he has dominated more than just politics, making his presence felt in almost every aspect of everyday life. He looms large in a wider context, too, figuring prominently in American political debate and enjoying mythic status among millions of sympathisers across Latin America and the Caribbean. He leaves few people indifferent; he inspires either genuine admiration or deep animosity. He is now the longest-serving political leader in the world, outliving such veterans as Paraguay's General Stroessner or North Korea's Kim Il Sung. Yet when he came to power in 1959, he was the world's youngest head of government.

# FIDEL CASTRO

1926–

CUBA

Fidel Castro Ruz was born in Oriente Province, the third of seven children. His father was a Spanish migrant and self-made man, who had achieved some prosperity in the sugar industry, and his mother a former household servant. After primary education at a local school, Castro was sent to a private Catholic school in Santiago de Cuba, where he received a disciplined formal education from Jesuit priests, and from there went to the prestigious Belén school in Havana. He was reportedly a rebellious youth, already resentful of American meddling in Cuban politics and attached to the memory of freedom fighter José Martí.

In 1945, Castro went to study law at the University of Havana and became deeply involved in Cuba's volatile politics. He joined the left-of-centre Orthodox Party and began to travel abroad in the pursuit of radical causes. In 1947, he was implicated in an unsuccessful coup against the dictator of the Dominican Republic, Leonidas Trujillo, and in 1948 he was in Bogotá, Colombia, when an insurrection broke out following the murder of a liberal politician. After witnessing what he believed were rigged elections later that year, Castro made a bid for the leadership of the Orthodox Party. In 1952, Fulgencio Batista took power by overthrowing the civilian government, confirming Castro's growing belief that democratic elections were irrelevant to Cuba.

Plotting against Batista's dictatorship, Castro risked imprisonment or worse, but on July 26, 1953, he and 150 revolutionaries attacked the Moncada barracks in Santiago. Hugely outnumbered, they failed and Castro was condemned to 15 years imprisonment for conspiracy. His courtroom speech, known as *History Will Absolve Me*, was an eloquent attack on Batista, and it earned Castro a reputation as an orator and idealist. Finally released under the terms of an amnesty in May 1955, Castro left for Mexico with one aim in mind: to plan the armed overthrow of Batista's regime.

In exile, Castro recruited a small group of revolutionaries, committed to the idea of a new insurrection. The theory of the guerrilla vanguard, as developed by Ernesto 'Che' Guevara, was that Cuba's peasantry would join the armed revolutionaries in a

*Fidel Castro (right) with Ernesto 'Che' Guevara*

much wider rebellion. With this strategy in place, the 82 revolutionaries set sail aboard the *Granma*, heading for the south-eastern coast of Cuba. There, however, they were awaited by Batista's forces, and only 12 guerrillas, including Castro, his brother Raúl and Guevara escaped into the mountains of the Sierra Maestra.

From his mountain stronghold Castro transformed this small band into the nucleus of a revolutionary army. Gradually winning peasant support and engaging the regular army in hit-and-run guerrilla attacks, Castro's force contributed substantially to Batista's growing crisis. When the US withdrew its support for the dictatorship, Castro's troops were able to overrun the demoralised Cuban military, and on January 1, 1959 he and his bearded fighters entered a jubilant Havana.

At first, Castro promised elections and a commitment to the liberal 1940 Constitution. But his radicalism soon began to alarm his moderate allies, and in 1961, he cancelled forthcoming elections and pronounced Cuba a socialist state. At this point he was nominally head of the armed forces, but in reality he directly oversaw a sweeping programme of reform, including the dismantling of large rural estates and the nationalisation of foreign assets. The changes were indeed revolutionary, and Che Guevara, in charge of much economic policy, advocated the replacement of personal profit with the utopian ideal of the 'New Man', by which workers would act only for the good of all. The government made huge investments in health and education, but dissent was also fiercely repressed by what critics described as a police state.

The US was deeply alarmed at these developments. Imposing an embargo and then backing the abortive anti-Castro invasion at the Bay of Pigs in April 1961, Washington only managed to deepen Castro's already deep dislike of American 'imperialism'. As a consequence, he looked elsewhere for financial and ideological support and found it in the Soviet Union. An influx of Soviet aid in the 1960s and 1970s underpinned the island's shaky economy but also made it dependent on Moscow.

While Castro survived various attempts by the US to assassinate or overthrow him, he presided over an erratic economic policy. Early attempts to reduce Cuban dependence on sugar were abandoned once the island began trading sugar against Soviet oil. Some elements of economic liberalisation were occasionally tolerated, such as private farmers' markets, but then suddenly withdrawn. The imposition of five- and ten-year plans swelled the ranks of the party bureaucracy, and the US embargo starved the island of desperately needed goods and markets.

Through the 1970s and 1980s, Cuba built an international reputation out of all proportion to its size. The sending of troops to southern Africa and high-profile support for left-wing governments in Nicaragua and Grenada, won Castro considerable support internationally as well as ever mounting hostility from the US. Alleged human rights abuses, a flood of refugees and a stream of nationalistic rhetoric ensured that Castro was one of Washington's main cold war bogeymen.

But Castro's fortunes and the future of the Cuban Revolution were suddenly thrown into jeopardy in 1989 with the collapse of the Soviet Union and the abrupt ending of Soviet support. Faced with economic disaster, Castro remained defiant in a series of characteristically fiery speeches:

> We should not be discouraged by these difficulties, nor those stemming from objective conditions in the world today, in which thousands of millions of people are plundered by neo-colonialist, imperialist powers . . . on the contrary, we should raise our voices in common struggle. . . .We should be prepared to face all difficulties and all aggression, to fight on every terrain.

*Fidel Castro, the revolutionist*

As a true survivor, Castro managed to weather the turbulent decade following the Soviet collapse. Increased austerity and growing popular discontent at times seemed to threaten his position, and there has long been speculation as to when he might resign from power. But Castro remains an unpredictable force, his unswerving commitment to his Revolution matched only by his ability to out-manoeuvre enemies and opponents. For a long time, he and his regime have been described as anachronistic in a post-Communist world order, but many Cubans are more fearful of what might happen after his departure than they are of further deprivation under existing circumstances. Castro is still convinced that history will absolve him, but when that judgment takes place is anyone's guess.

# LUCETTE MICHAUX-CHEVRY
## 1929–
GUADELOUPE

**W**omen in the Caribbean have traditionally faced enormous obstacles in making a career in politics. Ingrained *machismo* and old-fashioned prejudice have, for the most part, ensured that politics remains a man's world. Many of the values and attitudes that are considered essential to a successful politician's character – ruthless ambition, cunning, singlemindedness – are not normally associated with women, least of all by women themselves.

But there are exceptions to this rule. The Cuban Revolution, for instance, with its radical redefinition of gender roles, pushed some women towards the top of the political system, even if few reached the upper echelons of the Communist hierarchy.

In Guyana, Janet Jagan, an American-born dentist and widow of the veteran Cheddi Jagan, was the country's first woman prime minister and president in 1997. Yet altogether more long-lasting was Dominica's own Iron Lady, a Caribbean version of Margaret Thatcher, whose conservative views were strongly held. A lawyer by training, Dame Eugenia Charles was prime minister from 1980 to 1995 and a force to be reckoned with.

Guadeloupe, too, has a *dame de fer* or Iron Lady, in the form of Lucette Michaux-Chevry, who has played a central role in the island's politics for the best part of a half a century. Born on March 5, 1929 in Saint-Claude, she received a degree in Law from the Sorbonne in 1954 and was later called to the Bar in Guadeloupe. Her political trajectory began three years later when she was elected Municipal Councillor for Saint-Claude, and from then she steadily climbed the ladder until in 1982 she was elected Chairman of the General Council. From this position she worked tirelessly to restructure the island's relationship with France, especially by decentralising operations between Paris and the island's administrative capital Basse-Terre. It was also during this period that she caught the attention of Jacques Chirac, who opened doors for her in government in Paris.

The year 1986 marked a milestone for Lucette Michaux-Chevry as she was elected *député* for the island and at the same time was nominated State Secretary in the Office of the Prime Minister in charge of *Francophonie*, in other word's France's relations with the reset of the French-speaking world. While occupying these positions, she was guided by two main principles – a defence of national identity and a new form of international solidarity. In this sense, she became an ambassador for French language and culture throughout the world. In 1987 she became Mayor of the Guadeloupean community of Gourbeyre as a candidate of Chirac's Rassemblement pour la République (RPR) as well as Chairman of the Regional Council.

# IDEALS AND
# VISIONS

*José Martí*

(Cuba)

*Marcus Garvey*

(Jamaica)

*Theophilus Marryshow*

(Grenada)

*C.L.R. James*

(Trinidad and
Tobago)

Pragmatism and compromise are the day-to-day realities of politics in the Caribbean. Election times bring grand gestures and extravagant promises, but the ordinary business of government or opposition rarely rises above the mundane. Grandiose ideas can make a politician vulnerable and are best kept quiet. Cynicism can also enter into public life. The temptations of corruption are all too apparent, and many a politician who took power with the best of intentions can succumb to the lure of easy money. Nor has the Caribbean been spared the spectacle of rigged elections, of votes bought with a few dollars or a bottle of rum.

In this sense, the political ethos of the region is no different from anywhere else in the world. And yet if the rest of the world has produced political thinkers and statesmen of iconic status such as Mahatma Gandhi or Nelson Mandela, the Caribbean, too, has given birth to its share of idealists and visionaries, whose ideas transcended the ordinariness of conventional politics. In many cases, their ideas were ahead of their time; they often faced ridicule or hostility from those in power. But several Caribbean-born thinkers and activists have left an indelible mark not just on the region, but in the wider world.

The passion and integrity of José Martí are still venerated today in Cuba, the island he strived to free from foreign control. An ardent nationalist like many of his contemporaries, Martí was also a committed internationalist, viewing the whole of Latin America and the Caribbean as a single cultural entity. In the same way as the great South American liberator Simón Bolívar, Martí viewed the divisions between the territories of the Caribbean as artificial, as the product of imperialism and colonialism. He was also a true visionary in that he predicted that the freedom of his native Cuba would inevitably be compromised by the power of the US. The words and actions of Martí have inspired succeeding generations of anti-imperialist fighters, not least the guerrilla army of Fidel Castro in the 1950s.

Perhaps the most influential Caribbean figure of the twentieth century was Marcus Garvey, whose vision of a unified and independent Africa welcoming back its dispersed children from around the globe enthused millions of black people in every continent. Garvey's vision was utterly revolutionary, challenging the European stranglehold on Africa and calling into question the nature of colonial rule worldwide. Based on his own bitter experience of racism in Jamaica and his observation of exploitation in the plantations of Central America, Garvey's gospel of black redemption was religious in its appeal and subversive in its implications. Not surprisingly, the US and British authorities did their best to discredit him and to defuse his movement. Ridiculed and persecuted, he remained a courageous and consistent spokesman for black consciousness and the dignity of the African continent. Although Garvey died a broken man, his ideals have survived him, not least among the proponents of Rastafari and pan-Africanism.

Others from the Caribbean shared Garvey's ideal of a regenerated and free Africa. Edward Wilmot Blyden, for instance, born in St Thomas in the Virgin Islands, emigrated to Liberia in 1850, becoming the founder of that country's education system and its ambassador to Britain and France. George Padmore, born as Malcolm Nurse in Trinidad, devoted his life to the independence of Africa and died in newly independent Ghana. More recently, Stokely Carmichael, also born in Trinidad, won notoriety in the 1960s as a Black Panther in the US before going to live as Kwame Touré in Guinea.

Another advocate of unity, albeit on a more modest scale, was Theophilus Marryshow, the leading campaigner for Caribbean integration in the twentieth century. Marryshow rejected the 'small-island mentality' that has plagued the Caribbean since time immemorial and advocated a political and economic union that would transform a string of small and medium-sized territories into a single state. His dream almost came to fruition with the founding of the federation of the West Indies, but in the end pragmatism and *realpolitik* triumphed over the ideal of a united Caribbean.

The life and career of C.L.R. James are proof that political idealism does not necessarily fade with age. Throughout his life, James resolutely radical in his views, opposing what he saw as economic and political exploitation, not just in the Caribbean, but in the US and Africa. A brilliant historian, he told the story of the Haitian revolution and Toussaint L'Ouverture with verve and with a political message: that freedom from colonial repression could be won by force of arms. But James was no wild-eyed student revolutionary. He was actively involved with the ill-fated Federation, was a confidant of Nkrumah in Ghana and spent a lifetime teaching and writing on the subjects of black liberation and Marxist philosophy. He was also arguably the greatest of all writers on a sport not normally associated with revolutionaries: cricket.

His distinctive moustache and mournful features are impossible to miss in Havana or any other Cuban city. On posters, murals and postage stamps, this Victorian-looking gentleman, in starched collar and frockcoat, has an iconic value matched only by Che Guevara. José Martí is Cuba's national hero, a symbol of the country's struggle for independence and a byword for patriotic values. A poet, journalist and political activist, he was instrumental in leading the struggle against Spanish rule and also predicted the role that the US would play in Cuban affairs.

Born in Havana to a Spanish father and a mother from the Canary Islands, José Julián Martí y Pérez attended the city's San Pablo college, where he came under the influence of Rafael María de Mendive, a strong supporter of Cuban independence. While still a schoolboy he founded a newspaper, *Patria Libre*, the contents of which led him into trouble with the Spanish authorities. In 1869, he was sentenced to six years in prison, briefly imprisoned and then exiled to Spain. There he continued his verbal attack on Spanish colonialism while studying law at Zaragoza University.

# JOSÉ MARTÍ
## 1853–1895
CUBA

In 1875, Martí moved to Mexico City where he was reunited with his family and began his career as a writer. From there he went to Guatemala and then in 1878 to Cuba under the terms of a general amnesty, but he was soon expelled once more by the colonial authorities for involvement in pro-independence conspiracy. After further restless travelling, Martí finally settled in New York in 1881, where he lived for the next 14 years. In the meantime, the first ten-year War of Independence (1868–78), fought by Cuban guerrillas against the Spanish army, had ended in defeat. Martí, like other Cuban patriots, was determined to continue the fight. Cuba, together with Puerto Rico, was now the last Spanish colony in the entire Americas.

New York at that time was a hotbed of anti-Spanish feeling among the large exiled Cuban population. Martí, a persuasive and inspiring speaker, soon became an influential leader, founding the Cuba Revolutionary Committee, pledged to win independence for the island. He was able to unify the divided Cuban community in a way that nobody before had been able to, by emphasising that compatriots of all classes and races should fight together in the cause of freedom and equality. In particular, he believed that the black working class, especially the tobacco workers who had migrated to find work, should be at the centre of the struggle. At the same time, he continued to write tirelessly, publishing two collections of poetry and hundreds of articles in various newspapers. His poetry was simple, sincere and idealistic:

I cultivate a white rose
In July as in January
For the sincere friend
Who gives me his hand frankly.

And for the cruel person who tears out
The heart with which I live,
I cultivate neither nettles nor thorns:
I cultivate a white rose.

While living in New York, Martí developed a dislike and distrust of what he saw as US imperialism. 'I have lived inside the monster', he wrote, 'and know its entrails.' He was critical of US society and its striking inequalities, observing that 'democracy has been corrupted and undermined and has given birth to menacing poverty and hatred.' He particularly feared – and here he was indeed a visionary – that the US would take advantage of the anti-Spanish struggle in Cuba to impose its own influence. 'Once the US is in Cuba', he asked, 'who will get it out?'

In 1892, the Cuba Revolutionary Committee was turned into the Cuban Revolutionary Party, determined to fight what Martí called 'a just and necessary war'. He refused to become its president, preferring to be called merely a 'delegate'. Increasingly convinced that a protracted fight against Spain, like the unsuccessful first War of Independence, would play into the hands of the US, he began to plan for a swift and concerted armed uprising against the colonial forces. He toured various US cities, appealing to Cuban émigrés for money and support, and also visited Haiti, Jamaica the Dominican Republic and Costa Rica to win backing from sympathisers. In the Dominican Republic, he made contact with the veteran anti-Spanish fighter Máximo Gómez, and in Costa Rica with Antonio Maceo. Both men agreed to join forces with Martí.

Finally, in 1895, the insurrection plan was ready. Ships were waiting in Florida, loaded with arms and ammunition. After a false start in January, when the plan was betrayed and the US authorities confiscated the arms, Martí gave the order for the network of guerrilla groups to rise up across the island on February 24. He set off for the Dominican Republic to join Máximo Gómez and it was there, in the town of Montecristi, that he issued the revolutionary Manifesto, outlining the causes and objectives of the war.

Martí arrived in Cuba in mid-April, where he met Maceo. Significantly, the two men quarrelled, as Martí wanted the immediate creation of a civilian government, while Maceo proposed that the military leaders should have greater power. In the event, the dispute was never settled, as Martí was killed in a skirmish with Spanish troops at Dos Ríos, near Santiago, on May 19, 1895.

There is little doubt that José Martí, with his love of his country and people, would have been the first president of an independent Cuba. Instead, he is remembered for his unswerving commitment to democracy and to a region free of foreign control – *nuestra América* (our America).

# MARCUS GARVEY

## 1887–1940

JAMAICA

Marcus Mosiah Garvey probably had more worldwide impact than any other person from the Caribbean in the twentieth century. He was an inspirational leader, the founder of an organisation with four million members across 40 countries, and one of the first and greatest pan-Africanists.

Born in the rural seaside town of St Ann's Bay, Jamaica, the last of 11 children, he grew up in a poor family, his father working as a stone mason, his mother baking and selling cakes. His parents were devout Christians and encouraged an appetite for reading in their children. Until the age of 12, he had little idea of the significance of race and colour, as he grew up in a small community where a few white families mixed easily enough with the black majority. But then it was made clear to him that his early white friends were to be separated and sent to a different – and better – school, away from 'niggers' like him.

Leaving school at 14, he became a printer's apprentice before working as a printer in Kingston, where he led a strike for higher wages. It is said that he carried a dictionary in his pocket, aiming to learn five new words every day. He had written pamphlets and developed his political ideas before he left to travel around South and Central America in 1910. He later said that his first-hand experience of conditions on banana plantations in Panama and Costa Rica opened his eyes to the oppression suffered by black people in the Americas. At that time, there was a huge amount of emigration from the English-speaking Caribbean islands to places such as Cuba and Panama, where work was more freely available in the sugar plantations or in constructing the Panama Canal. The workers who left islands like Jamaica and Barbados often faced poor conditions and racism, and many died in Panama from epidemics of yellow fever and malaria.

There were several important influences on the young Garvey. His own experience had shown him that colonial Jamaica's education system was weighted against black children and removed all but the 'official' version of history from its textbooks. Jamaica's tradition of popular struggle, exemplified by the Maroons and the figures of Paul Bogle and George William Gordon, was not taught in the classroom, but it nevertheless lived on among the people as their unwritten history. Such ideas were strengthened in Garvey by Dr Robert Love, a Bahamian living in Jamaica, who was an outspoken nationalist and critic of the colonial system. Deeply unpopular with the white authorities, Dr Robert Love managed to win an election to the Kingston City Council in 1898, from where he spoke often of women's rights and the need to extend education to the poorest members of society. At the same time, black intellectuals such as W.E. Dubois, Booker T. Washington and the Trinidadian lawyer Sylvester Williams began to spread their ideas on black emancipation throughout the region.

These influences merged with Garvey's own direct understanding of colonial oppression.

When Garvey returned to Jamaica in 1914, after a two-year stay in Britain, he founded the Universal Negro Improvement Association (UNIA). The aim of this organisation was to campaign for equal rights and economic independence for black people and to create a united Africa to which they might one day return. Garvey believed that all black people, whether in the Caribbean, North America or Africa itself, formed one nation which had been broken up by European imperialism and which should be reunified. Garvey's slogan was 'Up! Up! you mighty people, you can accomplish what you will.'

In 1916, Garvey left for the US, where he built up support for the UNIA and created a newspaper, *The Negro World*. His influence was strongest in New York, Detroit and Philadelphia, but there were branches in Europe, Latin America and every Caribbean island. The UNIA ran a network of centres called Liberty Halls, which offered social services to black communities. It also supported a chain of black-run small businesses. Garvey taught his followers that one way to break free of discrimination and injustice was for black people to start their own businesses and hence become financially independent of the white establishment. But Garvey's most ambitious project was the Black Star Line, a shipping company intended to encourage trade among black entrepreneurs in America and the Caribbean. He and his followers bought three ships with this aim in mind, but was probably swindled in the process.

In 1920, the UNIA held its first international convention, and 25,000 people crowded into New York's Madison Square Garden. Uniformed members marched through the streets of New York, and the convention demanded equal rights for black people throughout the world.

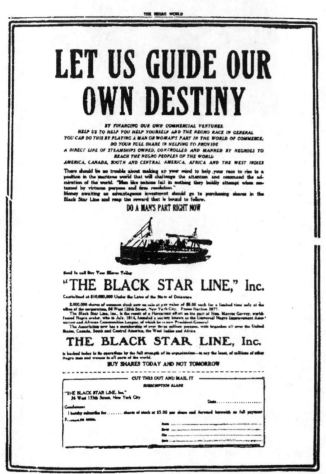

*Request to subscribe for shares of the Black Star Line Inc.*

At the heart of Garvey's philosophy was the idea of 'African redemption' and the powerful slogan 'Africa for the Africans!' Garvey believed that black people around the world should return to their ancestral African homelands, thereby escaping racism and beginning the reconstruction of a united African continent. It was soon known as the Back to Africa Movement and although the idea never really took shape, it exerted a powerful influence on many followers.

Such ideas were revolutionary in the 1920s, and Garvey gained many enemies. *The Negro World* was widely banned as subversive, and followers of Garvey were denied entry into several Caribbean territories. Some critics also accused him of being too

*Black Star Liner*
*Original artist*
*unknown*

interested in personal power and of encouraging a personality cult. Finally, in 1925, the US authorities arrested him on trumped-up charges of fraud concerning the Black Star Line and he was jailed for two years. When he was released, he returned to a hero's welcome in Jamaica, where he revived the UNIA and spoke to enthusiastic crowds.

> Therefore the American Negroes and the West Indian Negroes are one, and they are the relics of the great African race which was brought into the Western world and kept here for 300 years. I told them in Harlem that it was my duty to reunite the Negroes of the Western world with the Negroes of Africa, to make a great nation of Black men . . .
> (The Ward Theatre, Kingston, 1927)

Forming the People's Political Party, Garvey won a seat on Kingston's Parish Council, but the authorities prevented him from taking it up. They were alarmed at his criticism of colonial rule and his demands for improved conditions and wages for Jamaica's workers. He tried to seek election to the island's legislative council, but at that time only a small minority of people were entitled to vote. Those who were enfranchised were mostly from the upper and middle classes, and Garvey's radical ideas were anathema to such people. He lost the election and his influence began to fade. The UNIA also lost momentum, especially when the Depression of the 1930s created mass unemployment throughout the Americas. In 1935, Garvey left Jamaica for the last time, sailing to England where he died in obscurity five years later.

Garvey's remains were brought back to Jamaica in 1964 and he was made a National Hero. He is now remembered as a man who tried to instill a sense of pride and purpose in black people and as somebody who inspired following generations of civil rights activists and pan-Africanist politicians. Above all, he was responsible for creating an ideal and a dream shared by millions of people across the world.

# THEOPHILUS MARRYSHOW

## 1887–1958

### GRENADA

The dream of a politically united Caribbean has been shared by generations of reformers and visionaries, but it has proven as elusive as most dreams. The region is, of course, divided by history and language, with English, French, Spanish, Dutch and a range of local dialects separating populations who inhabit neighbouring islands. The political trajectory taken by countries such as Cuba and Haiti has often set them apart from the regional mainstream, while those territories that remain attached to their European metropoles – British, French or Dutch – have different priorities and loyalties to those of the region's independent nations. The Caribbean is an area of small or even 'micro' states, and yet even those which share a common language, cultural traditions and aspirations often seem unable, or unwilling, to work together.

There are exceptions; the Caribbean Community has done much to encourage joint initiatives across language and political barriers, while institutions such as the University of the West Indies or the Caribbean Development Bank underpin a sense of regional identity and purpose. The Organisation of Eastern Caribbean States, founded in 1981, successfully brings together seven small territories to promote shared policy in economic, defence and foreign policy. This is one of the first examples in the world of several independent nations sharing a common currency and judiciary.

But such regional achievements cannot conceal the fact that the ideal of a united Caribbean remains far from a reality. All too often, a 'small-island' mentality has prevented political leaders from sacrificing some of their local influence in the interest of a wider vision. The most important experiment in regional cooperation, the ill-fated Federation of the West Indies, lasted only four years, before it cracked under the strain of inter-island hostility and political cynicism. Abortive though it was, the Federation was as yet the most significant attempt to create a larger, potentially more powerful, political entity out of a divided region. It was also the culmination of the life and work of a man whose name has become synonymous with the ideal of Caribbean unity: Theophilus Albert Marryshow.

Born on November 7, 1887 in St George's, Grenada, Maricheau (he anglicised his name in 1907) was the son of a planter of modest means. His mother died when he was young and he was brought up by his godmother, the wife of Antonio Franco, a Madeira-born merchant. Franco managed to obtain the young 'Teddy' an apprenticeship as a carpenter after he left primary school, but Marryshow had other ambitions and in 1903 the influential Franco was able to persuade a local printer and publisher, W.G. Donovan to take on the boy. Donovan was considered a radical, and his newspapers such as *The Grenada People* advocated self-government for the British

Caribbean colonies as well as a political federation. At first, Marryshow worked delivering newspapers in St George's, but soon his intellectual abilities impressed Donovan, who promoted him to the post of compositor, then writer and sub-editor. Marryshow, for his part, was profoundly influenced by Donovan's progressive ideas.

At the age of 22, Marryshow was a respected writer on the *Chronicle and Gazette*, one of the region's best-known papers. He was also a conspicuous figure in local politics and in the Grenada Literary and Debating Society. In 1915 he joined CFP Renwick, a member of the traditional merchant class, in founding a new paper, *The West Indian*. As its name suggested, the paper took a strongly regionalist stance. In its first edition it promised to be:

> an immediate and accurate chronicler of current events, an untrammelled advocate of popular rights, unhampered by chains of party prejudice, an unswerving educator of the people in their duties as subjects of the state and citizens of the world.

*The West Indian* also looked forward to 'the day when, our islands linked together in an administrative and fiscal union, the West Indian Dominion will take its place, small though that may be, in the glorious Empire.' Marryshow did not envisage or demand complete independence (and few did at that stage), but his goals were certainly radical enough: greater representative democracy, improved working conditions for Grenada's plantation and manual workers and black self-empowerment.

As well as a journalist, Marryshow was an able politician and organiser. Under the slogan 'Educate, Agitate, Federate', he became in 1918 one of the founders of the Representative Government Association, a body which campaigned successfully for an increase in elected members in Grenada's Legislative Council. In 1921, he travelled to London to put the case for greater self-government to the British colonial authorities, while also speaking at meetings and conferences throughout the Caribbean. In 1924, Marryshow was elected to the island's Legislative Council, retaining his seat until 1957.

More a negotiator than a militant, Marryshow was instrumental in extracting reforming concessions from the British government, leading to gradual constitutional change. He rejected the political violence that swept through the Caribbean in the 1930s, advocating instead peaceful protests through the fledgling Grenada Workingman's Association. Although a consistent supporter of the rights of the poor, Marryshow was unable to form a viable trade union in Grenada. It took the advent of the firebrand union leader, Eric Gairy, in the 1950s to create the momentum for a strong union movement. Perhaps Marryshow was too moderate; the eminent historian, Gordon Lewis, judged that 'his staunch Whig constitutionalism never permitted him to fight the colonial power except on its own polite terms.'

By the 1950s, however, the colonial power was strongly in favour of a federal solution to the problem of running tiny and economically dependent colonies. The goal that Marryshow had advocated throughout his career suddenly seemed attainable, and the British, who regarded him as moderate and trustworthy, were happy to cooperate with him and his colleagues. After 11 years of meetings, conferences and consultations at which Marryshow was ever-present, the Federation was finally established in 1956, with elections held in January 1958. Fittingly, at the age of 71 Marryshow was elected by Grenadians as a senator to the federal parliament. He admitted that

> this is a dream come true. Today I am a member of an august body which I dreamed into existence.

Marryshow died in October that year. Perhaps it was fortunate that he did not live to see the destruction of his ideal. But that ideal survives today, and Marryshow's name is remembered with respect in Grenada, where his home, Marryshow House, is used by the University of the West Indies. During the period of the People's Revolutionary Government (1979–83) he was hailed as a national hero, and in 1987 his centenary was commemorated with a postage stamp. His greatest achievement was to popularise the idea of regional collaboration among the workers and farmers of the Caribbean by argument and political persuasion, thereby paving the way for future cooperative initiatives.

*Marryshow House, Grenada*

Historian, novelist, critic, political activist and cricket enthusiast, Cyril Lionel Robert James was born in Tunapuna, near Port of Spain, Trinidad on January 4, 1901. The son of a schoolteacher and book-loving mother, he was brought up surrounded by the works of Shakespeare and Thackeray. He did well at school, won a scholarship at the prestigious Queen's Royal College and became a teacher himself at the age of 19. He never lost his gift for teaching and was a sought-after lecturer and adviser for the whole of his life. Among his early pupils was the young Eric Williams, later to become independent Trinidad's first prime minister. James was also a keen cricketer and athlete, winning Trinidad's high jump championship.

Like many Caribbean intellectuals of his generation, James found colonial island life constricting and frustrating. His academic excellence was undoubted, but he still faced the barriers imposed by class and colour. In 1932, he left for Britain, to join his friend Learie Constantine, then a professional cricketer in Lancashire. It was the decisive step in his political development, as from the outside he was able to analyse the current situation in the Caribbean and increase his awareness of other issues. He found work as a cricket correspondent on the *Manchester Guardian,* but soon moved to London, where he was active in the growing pan-African movement.

# C.L.R. JAMES
## 1901–1989
### TRINIDAD AND TOBAGO

James was in his element in the political ferment of 1930s London. His contacts included orthodox communists such as George Padmore, Moscow's chief agent in charge of African and pan-African affairs, and a wide variety of Trotskyists and other revolutionaries. With other intellectuals and activists, he debated the role of Marcus Garvey, the importance of the Harlem Renaissance and the revolutionary ideas of *négritude,* then being developed in Paris by writers such as Aimé Césaire and Léopold Senghor. It has been rightly said of his tremendous ability that 'his intellectual frontiers were never closed.' His influence among radical black thinkers, nationalists and Marxists, was enormous. His publisher, Frederick Warburg, recalled: 'If politics was his religion and Marx his god, if literature was his passion and Shakespeare his prince among writers, cricket was his beloved activity.'

In 1938, CLR James published *The Black Jacobins*, probably his most important book and required reading for anyone interested in the history of Haiti and the Caribbean. In it he analysed how the slaves of French colonial Saint Domingue endured an 11-year civil war to drive out their oppressors and found free and independent Haiti. Central to the narrative is the figure of Toussaint L'Ouverture, the former slave and master tactician, who was instrumental in ending colonial slavery. This is a great piece of historical writing, but it also had a direct political message for

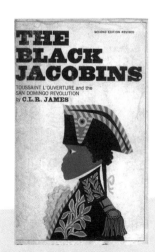

*New York: Random House, 1963*

53

the time in which it was written, for James was increasingly convinced that only revolution in Africa could end European colonialism there.

That same year, James moved to the US, where he became active in the Trotskyist Socialist Workers' Party. He was interned on Ellis Island in 1952 and was expelled the following year, returning to England. In 1958, he went to Trinidad and spent four years there in the period leading up to independence. During that time he was associated with Eric Williams, by now the leader of the People's National Movement (PNM). Attracted by the PNM's anti-imperialist stance, James became editor of the party newspaper, the *Nation*. Yet, within two years, he and Williams had split over ideological differences and James left Trinidad. From 1962 onwards, James was mostly based in London, where he died aged 88 in 1989. He was buried in the cemetery at Tunapuna, where his tombstone carries a quotation from *Beyond A Boundary*:

> Times would pass, old empires would fall and new ones take their place, the relations of countries and the relations of classes had to change, before I discovered that it is not the quality of goods and utility which matter, but movements; not where you are or what you have, but where you have come from, where you are going and the rate at which you are getting there.

James' stature as a leading twentieth-century Marxist thinker grew throughout his long and distinguished career. He was responsible for bringing together many different pan-Africanists, including Kwame Nkrumah and George Padmore. His intellectual curiosity encompassed many areas, including revolutionary politics, literature and, of course, cricket, and this helped him to place the Caribbean in proper perspective in world affairs. Africa – and the role of imperialism – remained a central theme in his thinking. He had no illusions about the challenges facing an independent post-colonial Africa, nor who was responsible for its many problems:

> Under the best of circumstances the future of Africa is a future of turmoil, stress and strain, revolution or counterrevolution, disputes between tribes and national units, complicated by the disputes between European powers and the Africans, and between the European powers themselves. It is a fantasy to believe that these imperialist powers are the ones who will guide Africa safely through these troubles. They are the ones responsible for them. They are the ones who are making it more difficult than ever for the Africans to find their own way.

A particular source of inspiration for James was Kwame Nkrumah, who became the first leader of independent Ghana in 1957. James visited Nkrumah on several occasions and perceived his government as a possible blueprint for independence across Africa. Nkrumah was ousted by a military coup in 1966, however, and James analysed his rise and fall in the book *Nkrumah and the Ghana Revolution* (1977).

James was always a passionate advocate of political independence, not only in Africa, but also in the Caribbean. As far back as 1932, he was arguing that Britain and the other European powers should relinquish their rule over the region. He was an early supporter of the concept of federation, arguing that the small islands should join together in a political union. Self-government, he said, was the only possible means of bringing democracy and freedom to people, and for this reason, although a Marxist, he opposed the one-party state constructed in the Soviet Union. James may be said to have ignited the spark of West Indian nationalism that would later illuminate the entire region.

A prolific writer, James's many works include the novel *Minty Alley* (1936), the play *Toussaint L'Ouverture* (1936) and a collection of political and cricket writing, *Beyond A Boundary* (1963). *Beyond A Boundary* was described by the *Sunday Time*s in London as 'the greatest sports book ever written'. Revealing James's deep love of the sport, it also uses cricket as a way of explaining Caribbean history and society. 'What do they know of cricket who only cricket know?' he asked, meaning that cricket in the region is much more than just a game. 'West Indians crowding to Tests bring with them the whole past history and future hopes of the islands', he concluded.

*Kingston: Sangster's Book Stores, 1963.*

# THE INTELLECTUAL TRADITION

**John Jacob Thomas**

(Trinidad and Tobago)

**Eric Williams**

(Trinidad and Tobago)

**Sir Arthur Lewis**

(St Lucia)

**Walter Rodney**

(Guyana)

For three and a half centuries after its first settlement by Europeans, the Caribbean was not a place where ideas flourished. Thinking was largely incompatible with the brutality of the plantation system, and slaves were hardly encouraged to develop intellectual interests. The small minority of planters, traders and administrators in most Caribbean colonies were not noted for their intelligence or curiosity. In terms of surviving the system, or perhaps escaping from it, instinctive cunning was preferable to intellect. Education, of course, was non-existent, apart from that provided for the children of the elite, but they generally preferred to go to school in Europe. Only priests and missionaries were allowed to take ideas to the mass of slaves, but these were generally ideas of resignation and humility.

A handful of religious visitors created what might be termed the first intellectual analysis of the Caribbean and its people. Bartolomé de Las Casas produced a stunning indictment of Spanish atrocities in his *A Very Brief Account of the Destruction of the Indies* (1551), while Jean Baptiste Labat, a French monk, wrote extensive and illuminating memoirs of his stay in Martinique at the end of the seventeenth century.

It was largely due to religious orders that the Caribbean's first schools were established in the wake of the abolition of slavery. Modest and under-funded, these establishments nonetheless played an important role in the spread of literacy and the encouragement of a rudimentary education for those children who were able to attend. John Jacob Thomas of Trinidad, was the product of such a humble establishment, he went on to become a respected commentator and to make an Oxford professor look foolish.

Gradually, schools for the urban elite were set up and expanded. Institutions such as lycées in the French islands and grammar schools in the British-run colonies educated the children of the growing middle class, while those from poorer but 'respectable' families were able to climb the social hierarchy by becoming teachers or joining the civil service. Some islands had particularly successful centres of academic excellence, such as Combermere in Barbados, Queen's Royal College in Trinidad and Jamaica College. One of the Caribbean's truly intellectual political leaders, Eric Williams, was educated at Queen's Royal College, as was C.L.R. James. Williams went on to guide Trinidad and Tobago to independence in 1962, earning an international reputation as a historian with books such as *Capitalism and Slavery*.

The brightest students in the decades preceding independence were able to win scholarships to study in Britain. Eric Williams (Trinidad and Tobago) Grantley Adams (Barbados), Norman Manley (Jamaica) V.S. Naipaul (Trinidad) and Sir Arthur Lewis (St Lucia). Lewis's brilliant academic career, in which he explored the potential and practice of industrialisation in developing countries, was crowned with a Nobel Prize for Economics, the first of two to be won by St Lucians.

The Caribbean has witnessed the emergence of several first-rank historians: Eric Williams and C.L.R. James, Philip Sherlock (Jamaica), Frank Moya Pons (Dominican Republic), Roger Gaillard (Haiti). One of the most exceptional was Walter Rodney, a controversial political activist, who was killed in 1980, allegedly at the behest of the then government in Guyana. The author of two classic works of popular history, Rodney was one of many left-leaning thinkers whose ideas have brought them into lethal conflict with the status quo.

The French- and Spanish-speaking islands have a long and reputable intellectual tradition, stretching back to the nineteenth century. Martinique is the birthplace of Aimé Césaire, and Frantz Fanon, the psychiatrist and writer whose revolutionary analysis of the Algerian liberation movement, *The Wretched of the Earth*, became a cult classic in the 1960s. Haiti, with a longer history of independence, has also produced several notable intellectuals, not least Jean Price-Mars, whose work as an ethnologist did much to validate his country's African-descended culture.

Cuba, both before and since the revolution, has been a place where free-thinkers have sometimes fallen foul of the authorities. But the island's mix of Spanish and African influences has inspired several generations of anthropologists and ethnologists, including Fernando Ortiz, the founding father of Afro-Cuban studies. Intellectual life, within the parameters approved by the revolutionary regime, is actively promoted in Cuba by institutions such as the Casa de las Américas, a cultural and publishing centre.

Both Puerto Rico and the Dominican Republic can claim significant figures in the fields of history and education. Juan Bosch, briefly Dominican President in the 1960s before a military rebellion unseated him, was a more successful historian and essayist than politician. From Puerto Rico came Ramón Emeterio Betances, a physician and abolitionist who campaigned against the Spanish presence in his native island and Cuba while at the same time writing learned treatises on the subject of cholera. His compatriot, Eugenio María de Hostos, was also a staunch opponent of Spanish colonialism, but his abiding fame resides in his championship of women's rights and in his attempts to reform the educational system in the Dominican Republic.

# JOHN JACOB THOMAS
## c1840–1889

TRINIDAD AND TOBAGO

The Caribbean has endured more than its fair share of foreign experts and commentators over the centuries. Some have come in search of the exotic, looking for colourful details or quaint customs with which to fill a travel book. Others have come to study the region's people, its economy, or its culture for academic purposes. Then there are those who have come to give their advice on the given problems of the day – from slavery and emancipation to today's drug smuggling epidemic. Most have been modest in their objectives, respectful of the people whom they met. Others have displayed the arrogance that goes hand in hand with being a self-appointed expert.

None was quite as arrogant as James Anthony Froude, the distinguished Victorian academic who graced the Caribbean with a visit in 1887. The eminent Regius Professor of History at Oxford, author of the acclaimed *History of England* and friend of Thomas Carlyle had become interested in the British Empire in the 1880s. He had visited South Africa and Australia and had concluded that far from needing independence, the colonies required closer ties with and firmer rule from London. Now it was the Caribbean islands' turn. After a quick trip around the islands, Professor Froude returned to England to write *The English in the West Indies*, which was published in 1888. Subtitled 'The Bow of Ulysses', the book likened the advocates of self-government to those suitors of Penelope, who were too weak to bend back the bow of the absent master, Ulysses.

Froude's argument was simple; the British had neglected their Caribbean colonies, and as a result the once-wealthy sugar islands were falling into disrepair and decline. The growing movement towards self-rule, he concluded, should not be allowed to succeed, since the colonial subjects were not yet ready to take over from their naturally superior masters. In short, it was an unremarkable exercise in late nineteenth-century racism.

It was also a book that caused a storm of controversy and resentment in the places through which the wise professor had fleetingly passed, for in the 1880s, the economic and political malaise affecting the region was encouraging many to question the nature of colonial rule. There had been little unrest since the Morant Bay rebellion of 1865 (more was to come in the 1930s), but the growth of schools, local churches and other social organisations since Emancipation had led to a greater self-awareness on the part of the impoverished rural majority throughout the region.

One man who read Froude's treatise with particular disgust was John Jacob Thomas, a product of that same self-awareness and an example of a true intellectual. Born in humble circumstances only two years after Apprenticeship ended in the British colonies, Thomas grew up among former slaves in rural Trinidad. The 1840s were a hard time in Trinidad, as sugar prices dropped and tensions grew between emancipated Afro-Trinidadians and the first indentured labourers brought in to replace them from India. Even so, Thomas was able to attend one of the earliest village schools and then went to a teacher-training school at Woodbrook near Port of Spain. Despite rudimentary conditions, Thomas became a first-rate teacher, imparting knowledge to the children of illiterate plantation workers in several ramshackle village schools. He also had a particular interest in the French-derived Creole spoken in much of the countryside.

Defying the colour bar in force at the time, Thomas rose quickly through the ranks of Trinidad's civil service, moving to Port of Spain in 1867 and then working as a Clerk of the Peace and Secretary to the Board of Education in the southwest of the island. A successful and efficient administrator, Thomas was also a passionate linguist. The fruits of his research into the language of rural Trinidad came in the shape of *The Theory and Practice of Creole Grammar*, published in 1869. It was a thorough piece of linguistic research, but also an important plea for the complexities of Creole not to be dismissed as a mere 'pidgin'.

A voracious reader and indefatigable letter writer, Thomas was an all-round intellect with interests in language, society and politics. Unfortunately, he also suffered from ill-health – rheumatoid arthritis – and was often bed-ridden and close to poverty. After years of illness, he eventually recovered enough to go to Grenada, from where he intended to sail to Britain where he wished to continue his research. It was in Grenada that Froude's book fell into his hands in early 1888. As a man who had spent his entire life studying Caribbean society and doing his best to improve it, he found Froude's glib racism insufferable. Immediately, he was moved to write a riposte and for fifteen weeks The *Chronicle and Gazette* published a series of his articles, countering Froude's opinions with devastating effect. Soon afterwards Thomas set sail for London.

The idea of turning the articles into a book may have occurred to Thomas during the transatlantic crossing. In any event, he arrived in London with two books in mind, an updated and expanded Creole Grammar and his anti-Froude polemic, entitled *Froudacity: West Indian Fables Explained*. The fables, of course, were those propagated by Froude.

One last obstacle remained before *Froudacity* appeared. Worried that the book would not sell, the publishers demanded a contribution to the printing costs – a sum that Thomas could not afford. Subscription lists were set up in Trinidad and various other islands, and the publishers were duly reassured by the number of orders. The book finally came out in July 1889. But it was almost too late for Thomas, who was now suffering from tuberculosis. On September 20 that same year he died in a south London hospital, aged only 49.

It is interesting to compare the Eton- and Oxford-educated Froude with an obscure Trinidadian schoolmaster who was educated in a village school with no blackboard or books and to discover that the latter was by far the cleverer. *Froudacity* is a complete

*London: New Beacon Books, 1969.*

demolition of Froude's humdrum clichés about race and culture and a very witty attack on the professor's pomposity. At one point in his book Froude declares: 'In Trinidad, as everywhere else, my own chief desire was to see the human inhabitants, to learn what they were doing, how they were living, and what they were thinking about, and this could best be done by drives about the town and neighbourhood.' Thomas can hardly contain his derision:

> 'Drives around town and neighbourhood', indeed! To learn and be able to depict with faithful accuracy what people 'were doing, how they were living, and what they were thinking about' – all this being best done (domestic circumstances, nay, soul-workings and all!) through fleeting glimpses of shifting panoramas of intelligent human beings! What a bright idea!

Laughing at Froude's self-importance as much as his ignorance, Thomas successfully knocks down each of the academic's assertions and opinions, making the case in the process for greater self-government and self-respect rather than the patronising paternalism of the Empire and its apologists. Froude's claim that the people of the Caribbean were unfit for self-rule was nothing more than 'bastard philosophising', concluded Thomas, and he added, for good measure, that the professor was trapped 'in the fatuity of his skinpride'. It is as one-sided an intellectual encounter as is ever likely to take place, and the winner was John Jacob Thomas together with his much-loved Caribbean.

Eric Williams was a comparative rarity in Caribbean political life: a successful politician who was also an intellectual. Few other intellectuals have survived long in the hurly-burly of local politics, but Williams left his mark on Trinidad and Tobago, dominating the country's politics for 25 years. Not only did he preside over the transition to independence, he did much to establish Trinidad and Tobago as a major actor in the Caribbean economy and regional politics.

Eric Eustace Williams was born on September 25, 1911, the son of a minor post office functionary in Trinidad. A bright child, he won a place at Port of Spain's Queen's Royal College and then an Island Scholarship to Oxford University. There he obtained a first class degree in history before going on to study for a Doctor of Philosophy degree, which he received in 1938. Already an outstanding historian in his twenties, Williams produced a thesis entitled The Economic Aspect of the West Indian Slave Trade and Slavery. It was this interest in the economic foundations of historical processes that marked all of his most important work.

In 1939, Williams moved to the US to teach social and political sciences at Howard University. While there, he continued his research into Caribbean history, publishing *The Negro in the Caribbean* (1940) and his masterpiece, *Capitalism and Slavery* (1943). This work argued convincingly that slavery and the plantation system were instrumental in providing the impetus for the Industrial Revolution in Europe and the birth of capitalism. It also demonstrated that the ending of slavery was much less the result of humanitarian agitation by abolitionists than the work of free-trade interests in Europe opposed to the economic inefficiency of slavery.

During the 1940s, Williams also worked as a consultant for the Anglo-American Caribbean Commission, a body set up by the US and British governments to coordinate policy in the region. In 1948, he left Howard University to work full-time for the Commission's Caribbean Research Council in Trinidad. Once back home, he began to take a more direct and active interest in politics, increasingly conscious of the need for self-government in the British colony. In 1955, he resigned from the Commission, opposed to what he saw as foreign-dominated interests, and launched himself into island politics.

One of Williams's most unusual and successful tactics was to inaugurate what he called 'the University of Woodford Square', a series of speeches and lectures that he delivered to his supporters and others in one of Port of Spain's main public squares. The tradition of public meetings in Woodford Square continued from 1955 into the 1960s, and was a means for Williams to communicate directly with the public, explaining his vision of an independent and prosperous Trinidad and Tobago.

Buoyed by the success of his lectures, Williams announced the formation of a new

# ERIC WILLIAMS
## 1911–1981
### TRINIDAD AND TOBAGO

political party – the People's National Movement (PNM). With him as its leader and intellectual inspiration, the PNM won a majority of the elected seats in the Legislative Council elections of 1956, under a new constitution offering greater self-represen-tation. For the next six years, as chief minister, Williams worked towards full independence from Britain, an objective he achieved in 1962.

Williams was also deeply involved with the ill-fated Federation of the West Indies, which came into being in January 1958 and lasted only four years. Grouping almost all the English-speaking islands of the Caribbean into a single political unit, the Federation was intended to create a new country stretching from Jamaica to Trinidad with a centralised government structure. Although the Federal Parliament was based in Port of Spain, Williams, like other island leaders, seemed ambivalent, fearful that his growing political power would be diluted within the larger grouping. Jamaica, in particular, was hostile to the federal ideal, claiming that smaller, poorer islands would depend on their larger neighbours. In 1961, Jamaicans voted in a referendum to quit the Federation and the project collapsed. 'One from ten leaves zero', said Williams wrily.

The collapse of the federation ushered in independence in 1962 and strengthened the PNM's grasp on power. A strongly nationalist party, it vehemently opposed foreign interference in Trinidad and Tobago's internal affairs, demanding, for instance, that the US military abandon its naval base in Chaguaramas, Trinidad. It also wanted to build up the country's economic strength, based on oil and gas, by using revenues to create new industries. But for some critics, the PNM did not do enough to assist the poorest levels of society. With its support firmly rooted among urban Afro-Trinidadians, the party was also accused of being indifferent to Trinidad's large, mostly rural, East Indian population.

Williams did not accept such criticism easily. Throughout the 1960s and 1970s, he controlled the PNM ruthlessly, expelling dissidents such as C.L.R. James, who believed that the party was not radical enough. Known as 'the Doctor', he developed a reputation for aloofness and arrogance. The so-called 1970 'Black Power' uprising, leading to strikes and looting, shook him badly, but he refused to make concessions to the young radicals behind it.

Then, in 1973, Trinidad and Tobago became the beneficiary of an extraordinary oil windfall, as world petroleum prices quadrupled. For almost ten years the country was awash with petrodollars and experienced a dramatic boom. Williams, was more distressed than pleased by the oil boom, disappointed by his people's materialism and greed. He died on March 29, 1981, a lonely and apparently disillusioned figure.

Eric Williams is best remembered as a first-rate historian and writer, whose intellectual prowess was matched by great readability. Take this paragraph from his seminal history, *From Columbus to Castro* (1969):

> Gold, sugar, slaves, this Caribbean trinity represented an enormous accession of wealth and power. Not surprisingly, Spain's imperialist rivals insisted on their share. The Caribbean islands began their association with modern society as the pawn of European power politics, the cockpit of Europe, the arena of Europe's wars hot and cold.

*Kingston: Ian Randle Publishers, 2004; Chapel Hill: University of North Carolina Press, 1994.*

# SIR ARTHUR LEWIS

## 1951–1991

ST LUCIA

The beautiful and mountainous island of St Lucia is banana country. In the lush valleys stand vast, regimented plantations of banana trees, while on precipitous hillsides, small clusters of fruit-bearing plants cling to the soil. Bananas have been the mainstay of the island's economy since the 1950s, bringing modest wealth to thousands of small farmers who could always count on the weekly arrival of the banana boat from Britain and a cash payment for their fruit.

But bananas have also been a risky business. Hurricanes tear down the shallow-rooted trees, while disease always threatens. More hazardous perhaps are uncertainties in the world price paid for the fruit. For decades St Lucia's bananas were guaranteed preferential entry into the British, and then European, market, and with that came a certain stability in prices. But the objections of the huge US banana multinationals to what they see as unfair protectionism, backed by the World Trade Organisation, have threatened the whole of the Caribbean banana industry. Everybody knows that small farmers, backed by family labour, cannot compete with the giant plantations of Central and South America. Even so, what are the alternatives, ask the farmers?

Sir Arthur Lewis would have understood, and lamented, the present-day economic dilemma of his native St Lucia. For his intellectual contribution to the Caribbean, and to the developing world as a whole, was to warn of the risks of depending on commodities such as bananas at the expense of building a more diversified economy. The Caribbean, of course, has always been an exporter of agricultural and other commodities, starting with the Spanish gold rush in Hispaniola and moving through sugar, coffee, bauxite and bananas to the contemporary 'non-traditional' commodities of cut flowers and mangetout. What Lewis pointed out was that such reliance on a handful of crops or minerals condemns the exporting country to another form of dependence: on imported manufactured goods and services. In short, if the Caribbean exports only bananas, will it earn enough to buy cars and computers?

William Arthur Lewis was born in St Lucia on January 23, 1915 to parents who had migrated to the island from Antigua 12 years earlier. From an early age he showed uncommon academic ability, a gift that was strangely encouraged by an illness when he was seven years old. During that time he was forced to miss several weeks of school, and his father decided to teach him at home so that he would not fall behind in his studies. Over the next three months the young boy learned so much that when he returned to school, he was placed two grades higher. Later he recalled: 'So the rest of my school life and early working life, up to age 18, was spent with fellow students or workers two or three years older than I. This gave me a terrible sense of physical inferiority, as well as an understanding, which has remained with me ever since, that high marks are not everything.' The modesty of the remark was typical of Lewis.

Unfortunately, Lewis's father died soon afterwards, and his mother was left alone to bring up five boys. He left school at 14 and went to work as a clerk in the island's civil service, waiting until he was old enough to sit the competitive examination for the St Lucia government scholarship to a British university. This he did in 1932, winning a place at the London School of Economics (LSE) to study for a Bachelor of Commerce degree. At that time, Lewis actually wanted to be an engineer, but the colonial authorities operated a colour bar, and neither the island government nor the few white-owned companies would have employed a black person as an engineer. Not wanting to be a doctor or lawyer (the two independent professions chosen by the educated black middle class), Lewis opted for a subject about which he knew little.

Despite his lack of experience, Lewis was an outstanding scholar at the LSE, obtaining a first-class degree and then winning a scholarship to study for a doctorate in Industrial Economics. Even more unusual for a black student, Lewis was given a one-year teaching appointment in 1938, which was followed by other academic posts. By 1948, at the age of 33, he was Professor of Economics at the University of Manchester.

Early in his academic career, he received some important advice from Frederick Hayek, the chairman of the LSE's Department of Economics:

> I got into the history of the world economy because [he] suggested that I teach a course on 'what happened between the wars' to give concreteness to the massive doses of trade cycle theory which then dominated the curriculum. I replied to Hayek that I did not know what happened between the wars; to which he replied that the best way of learning a subject was to teach it.

Lewis was an outstanding teacher and a first-rate administrator, but he also had something original to contribute in terms of his own original thinking. After years studying economic cycles, the causes of the Great Depression of 1929 and the workings of the world economy, he published a series of articles and then a book, *The Theory of Economic Growth* (1955), which analysed the relationship between rich, industrialised nations and poor, underdeveloped countries. His conclusions challenged the orthodox view of the 'international division of labour', by which developing countries were supposed to supply more powerful economies with primary products in return for manufactured goods. He argued that even the smallest economies such as those of the Caribbean islands should develop their own industries, thereby reducing dependence on imported goods.

Some of Lewis's arguments caused a good deal of controversy. His belief that foreign capital investment could be used positively to build up local manufacturing was dismissed by some critics, who insisted that foreign investors, particular from the US, were interested only in exploiting local labour. What became known as 'industrialisation by invitation' became a contentious issue, as economists and politicians debated whether the influx of foreign capital could encourage sustainable economic development.

Meanwhile, Lewis worked as a consultant to various colonial territories and developing countries, including Ghana, Nigeria and several Caribbean islands. In 1963, he became a professor at Princeton University, producing a stream of articles and research papers on economic and development issues. But perhaps his crowning achievement in regional terms was his role in establishing the Caribbean Development Bank between 1970 and 1973. This institution, headquartered in Barbados, was instrumental in providing the local capital for development projects and for encouraging economic cooperation between the nations of the Caribbean. Today, it plays a vital role in transferring development resources from donors and lenders such as France, Britain and Canada to local projects.

Lewis's contribution was recognised first in 1978 when he was knighted and then, the following year, when he won, in collaboration with Theodore Schultz, the Nobel Prize for Economics. This was the first time that a black man had won such an award. Until his death in 1991, Sir Arthur Lewis remained committed to the Caribbean, acting as vice-chancellor of the University of the West Indies and tirelessly promoting the ideal of regional cooperation. Today he is remembered in the Sir Arthur Lewis Community College in Castries, St Lucia, in whose grounds he is buried.

# WALTER RODNEY

## 1942–1980

GUYANA

Political martyrs are not rare in the history of Caribbean politics. From the earliest rebels against Spanish colonialism to the protestors of the 1930s, the region has seen many men and women who have paid with their lives for their belief in freedom and justice. In the second half of the twentieth century, several prominent political figures, from the left of the political spectrum, were killed for their political convictions. The Argentine-born guerrilla fighter and Cuban revolutionary, Ernesto 'Che' Guevara, was executed by the Bolivian military as he tried to lead a peasant uprising in the Andes. Maurice Bishop, charismatic head of Grenada's short-lived People's Revolutionary Government, was gunned down by former colleagues in a bloody schism within the island's Marxist leadership. Jamaican dub poet, Mikey Smith, was stoned to death outside the local headquarters of a political party the day after he had heckled a minister from that party at a public meeting.

The death of Walter Rodney was yet another instance of the lengths to which established powers will go to prevent the spread of revolutionary ideas. Although the precise circumstances behind his demise on June 13, 1980 have yet to be fully clarified, it is not unreasonable to assume that Rodney's fearless and consistent denunciations of the then Guyanese government may have played a part in what happened.

Walter Rodney was born in Guyana's capital, Georgetown, on March 23, 1942. At that time the South American territory was called British Guiana and was a colony ruled for the most part from London. In the course of the 1950s, the movement towards self-government and eventual independence created a volatile political situation in which race played an explosive part. Since the mid-nineteenth century the colony had imported hundreds of thousands of indentured labourers from India to replace the African-descended labour force from the era of slavery. Two separate populations thus co-existed, mostly peacefully, but the question of political power led to the forming of parties along racial lines. In 1955, when Rodney was 13, the People's Progressive Party split along such lines, with the Indian population following Cheddi Jagan and the Afro-Guyanese population supporting the newly formed People's National Congress of Forbes Burnham. For the next decade, a mixture of race riots, British meddling and almost permanent instability wracked Guyana. In the end, Burnham emerged triumphant, sidelining Jagan for many years, and creating a near dictatorship from 1964 onwards.

The young Rodney watched political developments with growing unease. A gifted school student, he won a scholarship to Georgetown's Queen's College, and then a Caribbean scholarship to read history at the University of the West Indies in Jamaica. Having obtained a first-class degree, he won yet another scholarship, this time to the

School of Oriental and African Studies, London University. In 1966, he received his PhD in history. Although he was out of his native Guyana for much of this time, he remained very much in touch with events there. Nor was Rodney interested in an 'ivory tower' academic career. His research was historical, but it concerned the impact of the transatlantic slave trade on West Africa, and this led him to examine the historical imbalance between the wealthy countries of Europe and the exploited ex-slave exporting region of Africa.

After finishing his doctorate, Rodney taught for a time at the University of Dar-es-Salaam in newly independent Tanzania. Although interested in the social and political ideals of Tanzanian president, Julius K. Nyerere, Rodney returned to the Caribbean in 1968, hoping to work at the University of the West Indies. But by now, Rodney was an avowed Marxist and unashamed political activist. While teaching in Jamaica, he became openly involved with the growing Black Power movement and explored ways of working with the marginalised and, he thought, potentially revolutionary Rastafarian community. These activities did not endear him to the Jamaican government, which took advantage of his absence at a conference to bar his re-entry. Despite riots in his support, Rodney was banned from Jamaica. After a short stay in Cuba, he returned to Tanzania, where he lived for the next six years.

It was during this second period in Africa that Rodney wrote his most radical and influential book, *How Europe Underdeveloped Africa* (1972), a sustained critique of how international capitalism continued to impoverish the continent. It was a Marxist analysis, but not one clouded by jargon. Instead, like all of Rodney's historical work, it was fresh, readable and challenging. Writing 'history from below', from the perspective of the poor and the exploited, Rodney rejected conventional academic methods. This approach again formed the basis for what many consider his masterpiece, *The History of the Guyanese Working People, 1881–1905*, a study of class formation published posthumously in 1981.

In 1974, the University of Guyana offered Rodney the post of Professor of History, but the offer was later blocked by the University Council. Nevertheless, he returned to Guyana, giving occasional lectures and working on his research. More importantly, he threw himself into political activity, joining a party called the Working People's Alliance (WPA), which was explicitly non-racial in outlook and membership. He addressed meetings, travelling the length and breadth of the country and listening to the grievances of Guyana's workers and small farmers. His most central theme was that Guyana's poor had been subject to a deliberate 'divide and rule' policy, pitting African against Indian and thereby preventing them from seeing that they had much in common:

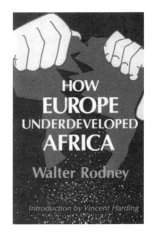

*Washington D.C.: Howard University Press, 1981.*

> You see, we have had too much of this foolishness of race. I'm not going to attempt to blame one way or another. I think more than one political party has been responsible for the crisis of race relations in this country . . . If we made that mistake once, we cannot afford to be misled on that score today. No ordinary Afro-Guyanese, no ordinary Indo-Guyanese can afford to be misled by the myth of race. Time and time again it has been our undoing.

Such ideas were treated with great suspicion by those whose power rested on maintaining the racial divisions in Guyana. And Rodney's charisma was also seen as dangerous by those who feared the emergence of a non-racial political movement. In June 1979, Rodney and two other WPA leaders were falsely charged with arson. This only led to a groundswell of support, and large crowds attended meetings addressed by Rodney despite overt intimidation from government agents.

On June 13, 1980 Walter Rodney was killed in mysterious circumstances that have yet to be explained. Given a walkie-talkie by an individual who claimed to be from the Guyana Defence Force, Rodney died when the device exploded in his hand, also injuring his brother Donald. The unidentified soldier immediately disappeared, and despite repeated allegations that he still lives in neighbouring French Guiana, the perpetrators of Rodney's murder have never been brought to justice. Forbes Burnham died five years later, his death finally opening up Guyana to a gradual restoration of democracy.

It is easy to believe that Walter Rodney would have been an even greater political and intellectual figure in Guyana and the wider Caribbean, had he not been killed at a tragically early age. As it is, he is widely remembered for his academic achievements and genuine commitment to the poor and excluded, irrespective of racial background, in his divided homeland.

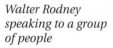

*Walter Rodney speaking to a group of people*

# THE NOVEL

*Claude McKay*

(Jamaica)

*Alejo Carpentier*

(Cuba)

*Jacques Roumain*

(Haiti)

*V.S. Naipaul*

(Trinidad and Tobago)

*Maryse Condé*

(Guadeloupe)

I t is a source of wonder that an area of the world with a relatively small population, a mixture of languages and dialects and a short experience of mass literacy has produced so many first-rate novelists. And the other extraordinary aspect of this literary profusion is that it is so recent. The Barbadian novelist, George Lamming, was guilty of only slight exaggeration when he said in the 1960s that Caribbean literature was just 20 years old. Certainly there were instances of regional literature dating much further back than Lamming's estimate of the 1940s, but it is true that the 'boom' in Caribbean writing did not begin before the 1950s and 1960s. Since then, the region has witnessed a steady stream of original and often critically acclaimed writing, from the 'magical realism' of the Spanish-speaking islands, to the bitter-sweet irony of English-speaking writers such as V.S. Naipaul or Sam Selvon. A further, vital dimension has been added by the cultural interchange between the United States and places such as Puerto Rico and the Dominican Republic – an interchange that has generated a group of Hispanic novelists writing in English.

The roots of the Caribbean novel lie primarily in protest and in a search for cultural identity. This was particularly the case in the Spanish islands, where a large European-descended population co-existed with a black slave population, creating a rich mix of influences as well as deep social tensions. Works such as the Cuban Cirilio Villaverde's *Cecilia Valdés* (1882) were sentimental attacks on slavery, while a novel like the Dominican Manuel Jesús de Galván's *Enriquillo*, published in the same year, was an attempt to create a fictional national identity based on the long-extinct Taino people. In Puerto Rico, Manuel A. Alonso's *El Jíbaro* (1884) lamented the eclipse of the class of white peasant farmers by large plantations and foreign capital.

Gradually, the development of a distinctively Creole sensibility, together with increased access to education and literature from abroad, inspired the first generation of modern Caribbean writers. Claude McKay, the product of a humble rural upbringing in Jamaica, came into contact with the Harlem Renaissance and made a name for himself as a politically committed novelist. In Cuba, Alejo Carpentier delved into his island's African heritage to find a rich seam of imagination and symbolism. The humiliations of US occupation in both Haiti and the Dominican Republic, meanwhile, encouraged an upsurge in nationalist sentiment and a revaluation of folk culture in writers such as Jacques Roumain and Jacques Stéphen Alexis, both of Haiti, and the Dominican Pedro Mir.

The post-war years ushered in a new, fruitful phase in fiction writing in the Anglophone Caribbean. Naipaul, Lamming, Selvon and others such as Roger Mais, Victor Reid and John Hearne (Jamaica), Michael Anthony and Earl Lovelace (Trinidad and Tobago), Edgar Mittelholzer and Wilson Harris (Guyana) added to the corpus of regional novels begun by trailblazers like Jamaica's Herbert de Lisser and Trinidad's Alfred Mendes. Many of these novels were commercial and critical successes, encouraging other Caribbean writers to get their work into print.

Today, hardly an island, however small, cannot boast of a writer of international stature. If St Kitts can claim Caryl Phillips as its national novelist, so Grenada can point to Merle Collins, or St Vincent to H. Nigel Thomas. In the French islands, the success of novelists such as Patrick Chamoiseau (winner of the prestigious Prix Goncourt for *Texaco*, 1992) and Raphaël Confiant points to an interest in the linguistic inventiveness of French Creole and the development of a multi-influenced cultural outlook known as *créolité*. This celebration of the region's unique mix of legacies is in some senses a development of what the Martinican writer Edouard Glissant described as *antillanité*, an aesthetic deriving from the Caribbean's multiform heritage.

Women are particularly prominent among recent and current Caribbean novelists. The tiny island of Dominica was birthplace to two well-known female novelists: Jean Rhys wrote the unforgettably atmospheric *Wide Sargasso Sea* (1966), while her contemporary, Phyllis Allfrey, produced *The Orchid House* (1953), an evocative account of the island's fading white plantocracy. Two Guadeloupean novelists are also well-known for their tales of Caribbean life and female resilience. Maryse Condé has been widely translated into English, as has Simone Schwarz-Bart, whose lyrical novels owe much to a culture of oral storytelling, fables and folk tales. Much of the best contemporary Jamaican fiction is now coming from women writers like Olive Senior and Velma Pollard. The most promising current writer with Haitian connections is Edwidge Danticat, who deals with the country's troubled past in novels such as *The Farming of Bones* (1999).

Exile and migration have long been potent themes in Caribbean fiction, with places as diverse as London, Paris, New York and Miami playing a crucial role in the evolution of a truly transnational literature. Writers such as René Depestre (Haiti) or Guillermo Cabrera Infante (Cuba) have spent more time in exile than in their native islands, while a new generation of authors – Danticat, Junot Díaz and Julia Alvarez (Dominican Republic), Rosario Ferré (Puerto Rico) and Cristina García (Cuba) – are largely resident in the US, while writing about the Caribbean.

Always evolving, always receptive to new influences, Caribbean fiction seems to be going from strength to strength. Its vitality and variety reflect those of the Caribbean itself and are perhaps signs that, despite its many achievements, it is still in its infancy.

Caribbean literature was late to develop, but this fact should hardly surprise us. For centuries, the region was dominated by the plantation system and slavery, neither of which was conducive to the encouragement of reading and writing. The earliest written work to emerge from the Caribbean was nearly always produced by outsiders – missionaries, travellers, merchants – who had been educated in Europe. The tiny majority of people born in the Caribbean who received an education normally did so abroad. As for the slaves and their descendants, literature was a matter of story-telling, of oral traditions passed down the generations.

It was only with the abolition of slavery and the founding of the first schools for the children of former slaves that a truly Caribbean literature became possible. Even then, few families had the money or ambition to have their children educated to a point where they could consider writing for pleasure or profit. It would take another half century before a writer from the Caribbean was able to find international celebrity and success, even if his fame was sadly short-lived.

# CLAUDE McKAY
## 1890–1948
### JAMAICA

That writer was Jamaica's Claude McKay, the first black writer in the world to produce a best-selling novel and to win an international readership. He was a poet, novelist and journalist and was also, for most of his life, a political activist involved in campaigning for black civil rights and social justice.

Born near James Hill in Jamaica's parish of Clarendon, McKay came from a poor farming family. His rural childhood is fondly recalled in the autobiographical *My Green Hills of Jamaica*, which he wrote many years later in the 1940s. Here, he recalls the daily rhythms of life in a small country community, more or less cut off from the modern world. But McKay read avidly as a boy, borrowing books from the mission library and reading neighbours' newspapers. Despite his poor background, he managed to gain enough education to leave the island in 1912 to study agriculture in Kansas. But McKay soon tired of studying and took a wide range of jobs – 'porter, fireman, waiter, bar-boy, houseman' – while writing poetry. He went to Britain in 1919 and stayed for two years before returning to the US where he worked on the left-wing magazine *Liberator*.

At around this time, New York was home to a group of black writers, whose literary and political movement was known as the Harlem Renaissance. Influenced by Marcus Garvey's pan-Africanism, they were interested in fighting racism and championing black cultural identity through their writing. McKay became associated with this group, and in 1928, his novel *Home to Harlem*, a realistic portrayal of inner-city life, was a great success. Some critics attacked the book as sensationalist in its portrayal of Harlem's black community, but it made McKay's name as a writer and sold 50,000

*Chicago: Charles H. Kerr Publishing Co., 1990.*

*Harcourt Brace, 1974*

*Why was he, a West Indian peasant boy, held prisoner within the huge granite-gray walls of New York? Dreaming of tawny tasseled fields of sugar-cane, and silver-gray John-tuhits among clusters of green and glossy-blue berries of pimento . . .*

copies. Another novel, *Banjo* (1929) and a collection of short stories, *Gingerland* (1932) followed.

During this period, McKay travelled tirelessly, visiting many countries in Europe and Africa. His fiction reflects this constant movement, and novels and short stories are set in such places as Marseilles and Morocco. He spent some time in the USSR, where he wrote a fierce condemnation of racism in the US, entitled *Trial by Lynching: Stories about Negro Life in North America*. This book was condemned as propaganda by conservative critics. It was also unusual in that it first appeared in Russian in 1925 and had to be translated back into English before it could be published in the US in 1975. At this time, McKay was supportive of communism and worked as a journalist for several left-wing newspapers.

The novel which deals most directly with Jamaica is *Banana Bottom*, published in 1933, the year before McKay finally returned to the US. It tells the story of Bita, a young girl who has been educated by missionaries in England before returning to her village, Banana Bottom. There she realises that her future lies with her rural community and she marries Jubban, a young farmer. In one scene, Bita joins in a dance and, as she dances, she forgets the education and training that have set her apart from her own people. We see her 'dancing down the barrier between high breeding and common pleasures under her light stamping feet until she was one with the crowd.'

Although it is a great novel, *Banana Bottom* was a financial flop, and friends had to pay for McKay to return to New York from North Africa. The economic recession of the 1930s meant that publishing was in crisis and McKay's early reputation had faded. He wrote an autobiography, *A Long Way From Home* (1937), but his publisher went bankrupt and the book made him no money. Forced to live from occasional journalism, McKay began to suffer from poor health. A final book, *Harlem: Negro Metropolis* was published in 1940, but was badly received by the critics and did little to restore his fortunes.

Eventually McKay was discovered, poor and sick, living in a Harlem boarding house. Helped by Catholic friends, he was baptised in 1944 and became a Catholic himself, renouncing his communist sympathies. He died in Chicago in 1948. Before his death, he was working on *My Green Hills of Jamaica*, his nostalgic recreation of childhood innocence. He wrote to a friend in 1946: 'My new book is about my childhood in Jamaica which is a source of inexhaustible material.'

McKay never returned to Jamaica after leaving in 1912, but a deep love for the island emerges from much of his work. In his short story, *The Truant* (1932), he describes a character called Barclay Oram who has left Jamaica for a new life in New York. The contrast between the idyllic Caribbean countryside and the city's heartless concrete jungle is one that McKay himself knew all too well:

Why was he, a West Indian peasant boy, held prisoner within the huge granite-gray walls of New York? Dreaming of tawny tasseled fields of sugar-cane, and silver-gray John-tuhits among clusters of green and glossy-blue berries of pimento . . . Why had he hankered for the hard-slabbed streets, the vertical towers, the gray complex life of this steel-tempered city?

From the 1960s to the 1980s, the literature of Latin America and the Caribbean experienced something of a 'boom'. The work of writers such as Colombia's Gabriel García Márquez and Peru's Mario Vargas Lllosa was very much in vogue in North America and Europe, and the term 'magical realism' was widely used to describe a new sort of fiction, based in historical reality but coloured by poetic imagination. The term was invented by Alejo Carpentier, a Cuban novelist of European extraction, and his novels, rich in both historical detail and exotic imagery, are among the best examples of the genre.

Born in Havana to a French father and Russian mother, Alejo Carpentier y Valmont was raised with a strong sense of his inherited European identity but also aware that he belonged to the Creole culture of the Spanish-speaking Caribbean. At the age of 12 he was sent to study in Paris, an experience which left him with a life-long affinity with the French capital. He returned to Cuba at the age of 17, studied music and architecture at the University of Havana (without ever finishing his degree) and then became a journalist. Mixing with a group of fellow intellectuals known as the Cuban Minority Group, he developed avant-garde and non-conformist ideas about literature and society, ideas that were to bring him into conflict with the

# ALEJO CARPENTIER
## 1904-1980
### CUBA

repressive Cuban government of the day. In 1927, his open criticism of the dictatorship of Gerardo Machado earned him a brief prison sentence; he was released the following year. By now, however, Carpentier realised that he could not tolerate the oppressive atmosphere of Machado's Cuba, and with the help of the French poet Robert Desnos, who was visiting Havana, he escaped on a forged passport to Paris.

For 12 years Carpentier remained in exile. While in Paris he associated with the surrealist movement, contributing to André Breton's journal *Révolution Surréaliste* and forging friendships with many of the leading poets and artists who were involved in the revolutionary reassessment of literature and culture in general. But despite his initial attraction to surrealism, with its rejection of conventional Western thinking, he soon tired of its iconoclasm, preferring to look back to the very different reality he had left behind in Cuba. In 1933, his first novel, *Ecué-Yamba-O!*, appeared in Madrid. Started during his time in prison, it was an attempt to bring to life what Carpentier saw as a neglected aspect of Cuban culture: Afro-Cuban religious belief. In his anthropologically researched piece of fiction, he recreated the life of a *ñañigo* initiate, Menegildo Cué, the practitioner of an African religion transported to Cuba in the nineteenth century. It was not a great success, but it pointed the way for Carpentier's later fictional masterpieces in its blending of historical reconstruction and poetic narrative.

Having worked in radio during his time in Paris, Carpentier accepted an offer to

ALEJO
CARPENTIER

THE KINGDOM
OF THIS WORLD

TRANSLATED BY HARRIET DE ONÍS

*New York:*
*Noonday Press,*
*1989.*

work as director of a Havana radio station in 1939, and for six years he was responsible for a series of cultural programmes as well as editing a newspaper, *Tiempo Nuevo*, and teaching musicology at the National Conservatory. It was during this period that a visit to Haiti inspired what was probably his greatest novel, *The Kingdom of This World* (1949), a dramatic and bizarre treatment of the events surrounding the slave revolution and its aftermath. With extraordinary imaginative power, Carpentier described the rise and fall of the megalomanic King Henri Christophe and his vast citadel in the mountains of northern Haiti. The cruelty of Christophe was proverbial:

Heavy-set, powerful, with a barrel-shaped chest, flat-nosed, his chin half-hidden in the embroidered collar of his uniform, the monarch examined the batteries, forges and workshops, his spurs clinking as he mounted the interminable stairways . . . At times, with a mere wave of his crop, he ordered the death of some sluggard surprised in flagrant idleness, or the execution of workers, hoisting a block of granite too slowly up a steep incline.

What fascinated Carpentier about Haiti was the explosive mixture of European and African traditions, exemplified by King Henri Christophe, with his Napoleonic uniform and belief in *vodou* spirits. A similar exploration of clashing cultural forces emerged from his next masterpiece, *The Lost Steps* (1953), which was inspired by another earlier trip, this time to the jungle interior of Venezuela. Here Carpentier tries to fuse indigenous myths with European story telling to explain the strange hybrid culture of Spanish-American society.

By 1945, Carpentier was once more alienated by the political atmosphere in Havana and he took a post teaching cultural history in Caracas, Venezuela. He remained in exile for a further 14 years, travelling in the meantime between Venezuela, the US and Europe. During this period he wrote directly about Cuba, and particularly its history of political violence, in works such as *War of Time* (1958).

But in 1959, the situation in Cuba was to change dramatically with the triumph of Fidel Castro's revolution and the departure of the dictator Fulgencio Batista. Carpentier greeted the revolution with enthusiasm and returned to Havana in June that year, ready to offer his services to the new government. With his international reputation already made, Carpentier was welcomed by Castro's regime and he was given high-profile posts, such as the vice-presidency of the National Council for Culture and a place in the National Assembly. He was also director of the National Printing Office, in charge of supervising what fiction and poetry was published by the state. Carpentier remained in revolutionary Havana until 1970, when he was appointed cultural attaché at the Cuban Embassy in Paris.

It is a matter of conjecture as to whether Carpentier finally became disillusioned with the Cuban revolution. Some claim that he was disenchanted with the censorship and secret police methods deployed by the revolutionary authorities, while others believe that he remained faithful to the idealism of the revolution. He never made a public pronouncement to either effect, but the politically cynical tone of his last novel, *Reasons of State* (1974), has encouraged the assumption that Carpentier had his misgivings about events in Havana.

After a varied and highly productive life in which he published not only many novels and short stories but also essays and a history of music in Cuba, Carpentier died in his beloved Paris in April 1980. His funeral in Havana was attended by President Fidel Castro. He remains one of the greatest and most original novelists ever to emerge from the Caribbean and has been an enormous influence on following generations of writers. Close to winning a Nobel Prize and honoured with many international tributes, Carpentier created a fictional universe in novels such as *The Kingdom of This World* that is as brilliantly vibrant today as it was more than 50 years ago.

# JACQUES
# ROUMAIN
## 1907–1944
### HAITI

For two centuries, since the country's bloody independence, Haiti has been made up of two separate worlds. The capital, Port-au-Prince, is a teeming, poverty-stricken urban sprawl, where the shanty towns of the many surround the hillside villas of the few. Here is the centre of government, the headquarters of the Church, the core of the economy. Everything from politics to football, from business to cinema shows, takes place in and around the capital. The other world is that of the countryside, of thousands of small villages and isolated farms, often unconnected to the wider world by roads or telephone lines. The majority of Haitians still live in the countryside, eking an ever more precarious living from farming smallholdings or working for larger landowners.

The desperate poverty of rural Haiti, made worse by the environmental disaster of tree felling for charcoal, has pushed millions into the slums of the capital or onto rickety boats bound for the promised land of Florida. Yet the two worlds remain very much apart. A small minority of light-skinned, French-speaking Haitians, living in the mountainside suburbs of Port-au-Prince, enjoy a large slice of the national wealth with their extensive business interests. The vast majority of the rural poor are black, speak only Creole and have few resources other than a small plot of land.

It was into this divided country that the writer Jacques Roumain was born on June 4, 1907. As a member of an old, wealthy and light-skinned Port-au-Prince family (his grandfather had been president), his childhood was one of privilege and comfort. As befitted a child of an elite family, he was sent to Europe to finish his education, where he spent several years in Belgium and Paris. When Roumain was eight years old, the US had invaded and occupied Haiti, claiming that the country's turbulent politics presented a threat to American financial interests and regional security. When he returned from Europe in 1927, the US occupation was still in force. By then, however, the presence of the Marines and the American administrators was beginning to attract widespread hostility among the majority of Haitians. A small guerrilla uprising, in which peasant fighters known as *cacos* attacked US forces, had been crushed, but resentment against the occupation was growing in strength. The young Roumain threw himself into the anti-American movement. A group of like-minded intellectuals issued fiery denunciations of the US and galvanised support among students. A student strike developed into a general strike in 1929, and that year Marines opened fire on a demonstration, killing many Haitians.

The experience of occupation and the ensuing withdrawal of the Americans had a deep impact on Roumain and others of his generation. Feelings of frustration and humiliation at a foreign occupation were accompanied by a pride in what they saw as authentic Haitian culture. The question of sovereignty, they argued, was inseparable from that of cultural awareness. Roumain was scathing about the imported, US-influenced habits of the elite; he was also dismissive of those cultural traits inherited from the French colonial masters. What inspired him was what he saw as the African-derived peasant culture of the rural population, with its traditions of collective work, self-help and spirituality. His early novels revolved around an ironic dissection of upper-class Haitian society, and in 1931 he published a short novel, *La Montagne ensorcelée* (The Bewitched Mountain), which told a dark tale of superstition and murder in a Haitian village. This was far from the romanticised peasant novels of some of his contemporaries.

But Roumain was also attracted to Marxism, and in 1934 – the year in which the US finally pulled out of Haiti – he founded the Haitian Communist Party. Socialist revolution, he believed, was the only possible solution to the enormous inequalities that prevailed in Haiti and elsewhere in the region. Like Aimé Césaire in Martinique and black writers such as Langston Hughes and Richard Wright in the US, Roumain was drawn to the Marxist interpretation of exploitation and racism. Such views inevitably led him into conflict with the conservative Haitian government that the Americans had installed. Roumain was arrested, charged with subversion and jailed; he was sent into exile in 1936.

During five years of exile, Roumain travelled widely in Europe, studying anthropology at the Sorbonne in Paris. When the Second World War broke out, he moved to New York and then on to Cuba. Finally, in 1941 a new government came to power in Haiti and Roumain was allowed to return. He at once founded the Bureau d'Ethnologie, a research body dedicated to analysing the country's peasant culture. He was also active in opposing the Catholic Church's 'anti-superstition campaign', a campaign against *vodou* (voodoo), the folk religion of the majority. Arguing that only a scientific understanding of society would eradicate the peasant's need for the supernatural, he insisted that an 'anti-poverty campaign' was the immediate priority.

In 1943, President Élie Lescot unexpectedly appointed Roumain as chargé d'affaires at the Haitian embassy in Mexico, probably as a means of reducing his influence at home. Roumain accepted, persuaded by the Communist Party, that he could advance their cause. It was there that he had time to devote himself more fully to writing. After a collection of poetry, he began work on his undisputed masterpiece, *Les Gouverneurs de la rosée* (The Masters of the Dew). By early 1944, the novel was finished, but on August 18 of that year, Roumain died suddenly in Port-au-Prince. He was only 38 years old.

*Masters of the Dew* was published posthumously; it was eventually translated into twelve different languages and has become an acknowledged classic of Caribbean literature. The

*Oxford: Heinemann, 1978*

*Washington D.C.:*
*Azul Editions, 1995*

story concerns the drought-stricken Haitian village of Fonds Rouge, its fields ruined by deforestation and soil erosion. Despair and fatalism reign, the peasants seeking consolation in rum and *vodou*. The hero, Manuel, arrives back in this, his home village, after years of cutting cane in Cuba and is appalled by what he sees. While falling in love with Annaise, Manuel resolves to remedy the village's problems by uniting its inhabitants in a common cause. He explains to his mother that as master of his own fate, even the poorest peasant can make a living from the arid land:

The sky's the pastureland of the angels . . . but the earth is a battle day by day, without truce, to clear the land, to plant, to weed and water it until the harvest comes. Then one morning you see your ripe fields spread out before you under the dew and you say – whoever you are – 'Me - I'm the Master of the dew!' and your heart fills with pride.

Manuel eventually triumphs when he discovers a hidden source of water and turns it into an irrigation system for the village. Jealousy and rivalry lead to his murder, but Annaise is carrying his unborn child, and the novel ends optimistically with the collective work of the peasants and the promise of new life.

Despite his tragically short life, Jacques Roumain made a major contribution to the understanding of Haitian peasant life. His critics accused him of producing Marxist propaganda disguised as fiction, but time has demonstrated the power and insight of his work. Destined perhaps to be yet another pale-skinned president, Roumain was the most important chronicler of the real Haitian experience. His novel is today as relevant as ever with its depiction of the country's ecological degradation. *Si ou gen youn sous k ap ba-w dlo, ou pa koupe pye-bwa kot-l.* 'If you have a stream that gives you water', runs the Haitian proverb, 'you don't cut down the trees around it.'

V.S. Naipaul's literary career takes the form – to use one of his favourite words – of an 'enigma'. He is without doubt one of the finest living writers in the English language, the author of many outstanding novels and a great deal of compelling travel writing. Yet his attitude towards his native Caribbean has always been, to say the least, ambiguous. He has written that the region has no history worth speaking of, that it has failed to create significant cultural achievements, producing rather the 'mimic men' who imitate European or North American fashions. But, paradoxically, some of his most successful works are firmly rooted in the same Caribbean culture that he has sometimes belittled. Arguably his two masterpieces – *Miguel Street* (1959) and *A House for Mr Biswas* (1961) – owe their enduring appeal to Naipaul's ironic, yet affectionate, dissection of day-to-day street life and urban existence in Trinidad.

# V.S. NAIPAUL
## 1932 –
TRINIDAD AND TOBAGO

Born Vidiadhar Surajprasad Naipaul at Chaguanas, Trinidad, he was part of a close family, descended from Brahmin Indian labourers who had emigrated to the island in the nineteenth century. His father, Seepersad, was a particularly powerful influence on the young Vidia, for he was a journalist as well as an aspiring writer, and he encouraged the literary ambitions that his son showed at an early age. Seepersad introduced him to a wide range of writers, including Shakespeare, D.H. Lawrence and Rudyard Kipling. Vidia was a promising student and in 1950 won a prestigious Island Scholarship to study English at Oxford University.

The move to Britain was to tear the young Naipaul away from his close-knit family and to expose him to the alien culture of an upper-class Oxford institution. The experience was at first traumatic, and Naipaul's letters to his family reveal a highly gifted individual trying to come to terms with his own identity. During this unhappy period, Naipaul came to view Trinidad with condescension while remaining aloof from the other students around him. The Oxford years reinforced Naipaul's ambition to be a professional writer, and it was while he was studying that he began to develop a clearer idea of what he wanted to write about. Naipaul had long known that he wanted to write; what was missing was the subject matter, and it was in looking back to Trinidad and his upbringing in an Indian family that he found his themes.

After Oxford, Naipaul began to write more or less full time, but he also worked on the BBC's 'Caribbean Voices' programme and reviewed books for the *New Statesman*. Finally, in 1955, the London publisher André Deutsch agreed to publish his first novel – *The Mystic Masseur* – which appeared in 1957. Naipaul produced a series of novels in the late 1950s and early 1960s, rapidly establishing a reputation as a versatile writer with an excellent grasp of dialogue and characterisation. Most of these novels were set in Trinidad, which he depicted both humorously and poignantly as a place of chaotically mixed cultural values and eccentrics. *Miguel Street*, is an affectionate

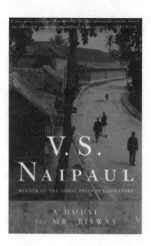

*Vintage Books USA, 2001.*

evocation of the rogues and dreamers who frequented the same world as the young Naipaul. But the real classic from this period is *A House for Mr Biswas*, a bitter-sweet tale of an Indian Trinidadian seeking to shrug off the constraints of a suffocating family life and looking to find his own independence in the form of a ramshackle house.

In 1961, Naipaul received a grant from the Trinidad government to travel in the Caribbean. The result was *The Middle Passage* (1962), a largely hostile and painful account of what he saw as the region's colonial or post-colonial mediocrity. 'History is built around achievement and creation,' he wrote, 'and nothing was created in the West Indies.' It was a negative assessment and one that marked a change in Naipaul's view of his birthplace. Further travel ensued as he visited Argentina, Africa, India and Pakistan and the US. Few of these places won Naipaul's approval, and he wrote pessimistically about the political future of a decolonised black Africa.

The fate of contemporary India has appeared consistently as one of Naipaul's deepest concerns. In his recent *Reading and Writing* (2000) he has described the country as 'the greater hurt', the other pain being that of Trinidad's cultural confusion. *In India: a Wounded Civilization* (1977) and *India: a Million Mutinies Now* (1990) he has traced his ancestral homeland's transition through independence, partition and immense poverty. Naipaul has also written widely on the impact of Islam on the modern world. Highly critical of what he sees as fundamentalist Muslims, he has argued that the imposition of Islam on converted countries such as Pakistan and Malaysia has involved the deliberate erasing of their cultural identities.

V.S. Naipaul has lived in England for many years and was knighted in 1990. He also won the Booker Prize for the novel *In a Free State* in 1971. In *The Enigma of Arrival* (1987) he depicted a writer of Caribbean origins who views his return to England after a long period of travelling abroad as a homecoming, suggesting that Naipaul now feels more at home in Britain than in Trinidad. His latest books cast light on the importance that the Caribbean holds within his personal and artistic identity. The publication of letters *Between a Father and Son* (1999) revealed the enormous importance of his relationship with his father and the struggle to make sense of his time at Oxford, while *Reading and Writing* underlined how his Trinidad childhood provided the material for his early literary success.

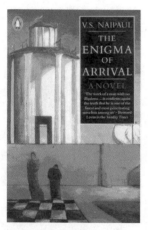

*London: Penguin Books, 1978.*

There remains a sense of emptiness at the heart of Naipaul's writing, a characteristic that has led critics to compare him to Joseph Conrad. In *A Way in the World* (1994) Naipaul once again returned to his childhood, trying to explain this emptiness in terms of his own lack of cultural identity:

> Many years later I thought that the feeling of the void had to do with my temperament, the temperament of a child of a recent Asian-Indian immigrant community in a mixed population: the child looked back and found no family past, found a blank. But I feel now that I was responding to something that was missing, something that had been rooted out.

This sense of loss, of a missing or false cultural identity runs through Naipaul's work, but in later years it has become more intense, more oppressive. It remains at the heart of his fictional world and provides one key to the enigma of this most rootless of writers.

In the title of their book on Maryse Condé (Ibis Rouge, 2002), French writers Madeleine Cottenet-Hage and Lydie Moudelino emphasise two of their subject's most notable characteristics – characteristics confirmed by many others. She is, they write, 'une nomade inconvenante', an unseemly nomad.

Maryse Condé is beyond any doubt a nomadic personality. She has lived in mainland France, in the African countries of Guinea, Ghana and Senegal, in the United States, where she teaches today at the University of Columbia in New York, and, of course, in her native Guadeloupe, where she was born on February 11, 1937. She often sets out to discover new horizons: Indonesia, Japan, South Africa, the Caribbean . . .

If her heart is a tireless traveller, she also likes to re-energise herself through regular stays in her Guadeloupean home of Montebello, replenishing her roots with the sounds, images and metaphors that lay at the core of the Creole language and which are at the centre of all local conversations. The creative tension between exploration and rootedness can be felt throughout her work. For instance the novel *Une vie scélérate* (translated into English as *Tree of Life*) takes us from Guadeloupe to Panama, then on to the United States, Paris and the

## MARYSE CONDÉ
### 1937–
GUADELOUPE

French city of Angers. The story is about Condé's own life and depicts the very events that have shaped her family. She herself describes this book as a long search for a Guadeloupean, West Indian, identity. Even so, the universe of Maryse Condé extends far beyond these notions, wide-ranging as they are. Madeleine Cottenet-Hage and Lydie Moudelino evoke a fictional universe which 'embraces vast spaces, not only from a geographical point-of-view, but also from a socioeconomic and ethnic perspective, covering a whole range of classes, colors, cultures and generations . . .'

She is also unseemly in the sense that she questions, reassesses, refuses to fall prey to any kind of prejudices or 'imposed limitations'. Antoine Compagnon, who nicknamed her 'the stubborn one', says: 'What I liked most about her was her complete independence, her rejection of watchwords, her fierce freedom of thought and speech.' This attitude is translated by the Guadeloupean writer Ernest Pépin as an assertive search for freedom: 'This is Maryse Condé's catchword: freedom. Not the kind of freedom which is weighed down by heavy dogmas, nor the kind of freedom limited by her race, her origins, her gender, but the absolute freedom which makes every human being a tragic and epic speculation.' It is not surprising, then, that she can sometimes seem provocative, a trait that enables Thomas Spear to underline the resemblance between the author and some of her characters: Maryse Condé can be recognised in her rebellious characters, the unsatisfied, the restless: Veronica (*Heremakhonon*), Romana (*Ségu*), Coco (*La vie scélérate*), Tituba, Spero (*Derniers rois*

*New York: Anchor Books, Doubleday, 1995.*

*mages*, translated as *The Last of the African Kings*) as well as several characters in *Traversée de la Mangrove (Crossing the Mangrove)*. The fact that her work, defying conventions, may seem to some as disturbing as herself, should not come as a surprise either. In this struggle for absolute freedom Maryse Condé includes the principle of some sort of independence for her native island, at least in terms of culture. In her opinion, there are too many external cultural influences, an opinion that led her to make an incursion into politics a few years ago.

With the help of Ernest Pépin it is easy to identify some of Condé's main themes. He writes: 'Maryse Condé's struggle bets on intelligence against all the entrenched forms of human stupidity which clutter the horizon of our century's end . . . For Maryse, the essential question is: which part of my legacy should I assume to get rid of all legacies? In other words, to be free to create both my future and my momentum. She realizes then that some legacies are rigged (*négritude*, Africa); some legacies are unacceptable (the condition of women); some legacies are fruitless (the sacrosanct question of identity); some legacies are concealed (the memory of the memorable) and that the only legacy worth mentioning is what Pavese calls "the hard work of living". Just as Nature knocks tectonic plates together, in the same way, Maryse Condé knocks our legacies against their fictions by shaking our convictions.'

There is no doubt that Maryse Condé stands as a point of reference for the literary world. A beacon, as Thomas Spear puts it. While recognising that she opens the gate to the lost ship, maybe also to the *bateau ivre*, the scholar admits that this metaphor clashes with Maryse Condé's globetrotting image. Nevertheless, standing firm on her rock, she lights the way for younger generations, both through her academic work and her literary works of fiction.

*New York: Viking Penguin Inc., 1987.*

# POETRY AND THE PERFORMING ARTS

*Nicolás Guillén*

(Cuba)

*Louise Bennett*

(Jamaica)

*Sidney Poitier*

(Bahamas)

*Derek Walcott*

(St Lucia)

The spoken word has a longer history than its written equivalent in Caribbean literature. The first poetry devised in the region, other than that by foreign travellers or a tiny leisured minority, was oral in form, taking the shape of work songs, satirical rhymes and call-and-response chants. All of these oral constructions were rooted in traditional African culture and survived the crossing of the Middle Passage and their transplantation into the Caribbean colonies. These were, of course, cultural survival mechanisms, reminding the slaves of who they were and where they had come from, restating their human identity amidst the dehumanising drudgery of the plantation. Initially spoken or sung in the languages of West Africa, these poetic forms soon adapted to the new influences, linguistic and conceptual, to which they were exposed. African languages became mixed with the English, French or Spanish spoken by the planters and overseers. Traditional spiritual motifs were fused with the iconography and beliefs of the Christianity that was intermittently imposed upon the slaves. Probably by the end of the eighteenth century, the undiluted African imports had disappeared, to be replaced by a synthesis of language and cultural references that was truly Creole.

The oral tradition has always co-existed with the written tradition, the one sometimes borrowing from the other. But for several centuries the 'official' literature of the Caribbean colonies tended to look down on the folk literature of their majority populations. Imported European concepts of metre, rhyme and imagery were largely at odds with poetic forms that emphasised the role of improvisation, repetition and topicality. Most of the poetry published in the nineteenth century was strictly classical in form and tone, with poets such as José María Heredia y Heredia (Cuba) and José

83

Joaquín Pérez (Dominican Republic) imitating contemporary trends in romanticism. Serious attempts to record oral poetry were not made until the end of the nineteenth century, but by then the double effect of emancipation and religious evangelism had changed the nature of spoken poetry forever.

Even with the advent of greater literacy and colonial education, however, the oral tradition survived across the Caribbean, handed down from generation to generation in songs, tales and poems. It took the arrival of a new wave of intellectuals and artists, sympathetic to their island's African heritage, to rediscover this tradition and incorporate it into their own work. One of the region's trailblazers in this respect was Nicolás Guillén, whose interest in his country's mixed cultural history was only matched by his commitment to the revolution of 1959. In Haiti and the Dominican Republic, young poets who were indignant at the US occupation of their homelands, also looked to folk culture as a source of national cultural authenticity. Haitian poets such as Emile Roumer and Philippe Thoby-Marcelin embraced nationalism and primitivism, exploring the contradictions voiced by their contemporary Léon Laleau:

> *Do you feel this suffering*
> *And this despair with no equal*
> *In taming, with words from France,*
> *This heart which has come to me from Senegal?*

In Jamaica, meanwhile, the patois poetry of Louise Bennett was proving to an ever wider audience that popular language was not incompatible with poetic expression. Her verse, comic for the most part but spiced with social observation, was performed as well as written, paving the way for a succession of performance poets such as Mutabaruka, Oku Onuora and Jean Binta Breeze.

In the Caribbean, the relationship between poetry and acting is a close one, with entertainers such as Trinidad's Paul Keens-Douglas and Guyana's John Agard specialising in a mixture of monologues and poetic sketches, often in dialect. As yet, however, relatively few Caribbean actors have won international fame, the main exception being Bahamas-born Sidney Poitier, who has starred in a string of box office successes. (Interestingly, Kelsey Grammer, also known as Frasier Crane in the popular sitcom *Frasier*, was born in St Thomas, US Virgin Islands). But films such as Jamaica's *The Harder They Come* 1973 (starring Jimmy Cliff) and the Cuban classics *Memories of Underdevelopment* (1968) and *Strawberry and Chocolate* (1993), both directed by Tomás Gutiérrez Alea, suggest that the Caribbean has a wealth of acting and directing ability, if not the resources of Hollywood.

It was fitting that Derek Walcott should have received the Nobel Prize for Literature in 1992, the quincentenary of Columbus's arrival in the Caribbean. It was a sort of official recognition that the region's poetry had come of age. In fact, a Caribbean-born poet, Saint-John Perse, had already won the Nobel Prize in 1960, but the Guadeloupean spent little time in the region after leaving as a child. Walcott's award was much more significant, for it honoured a poet who has consistently celebrated the culture and language of his native St Lucia, mixing the best of contemporary technique with the traditional Creole cadences of the Eastern Caribbean.

Poetry and politics do not tend to go well together. Nor do one-party states and creative writers tend to coexist happily. The Soviet Union was notoriously intolerant of any writer who decided to cross the narrow limits laid out by the ruling party, while communist China has actively persecuted dissident authors and thinkers. The Caribbean has also had its moments of censorship and subversion. Various Haitian dictators have imprisoned or exiled writers of whom they disapproved; the novelist Jacques Roumain spent several years in political exile, and René Depestre was unable to return to the country while the Duvaliers were still in power. The communist regime in Cuba has also had its differences with writers whom it views as overly critical or subversive. The poet Heberto Padilla found himself in court, charged with counter-revolutionary activity, before being exiled; the novelist Guillermo Cabrera Infante got into trouble with the regime in the 1960s and has been *persona non grata* in Havana ever since. Even Alejo Carpentier had a complicated relationship with the Cuban authorities towards the end of his life and preferred to live in Paris.

# NICOLÁS GUILLÉN

1902–1989

CUBA

Of course, there are always exceptions to any rule, and in this case, the exception is Nicolás Guillen, one of the greatest twentieth-century poets of the Spanish language and a faithful supporter of Fidel Castro's revolution to the last. Yet, it would be inaccurate to suppose that Guillén's communism determined all of his poetry, or that he was a mere propagandist. Some of what Guillén wrote, in poems such as *Tengo* (1964), was certainly intended to celebrate and popularise the achievements of the revolution in fields such as health and education. But much more of Guillén's work is concerned with wider themes: the cross-cultural history (*mestizaje*) of the Caribbean, its richly mixed Creole identity, and the legacy of its cruel history.

Guillén was born in the Cuban province of Camagüey on July 10, 1902 into a relatively prosperous family of mixed African and European background. His father had fought in the Second War of Independence and was a Liberal senator as a well as a journalist. Guillén's birth symbolically coincided with the year in which the Republic of Cuba was established, under the terms of the so-called Platt Amendment – a clause that allowed the US to intervene in Cuban politics to protect its own interests. Like his father, Guillén was to become a life-long critic of what he saw as US imperialism, as well as a thorn in the flesh of various dictators who ruled Cuba before the revolution of 1959. Guillén's father was to pay with his life for his political beliefs, for in 1917, he was assassinated on the orders of President Mario García Menocal, whom he had tried to overthrow.

His father's death had a profound impact on Guillén, who at the age of 14 became the family breadwinner. He trained as a typographer and then worked on the *El*

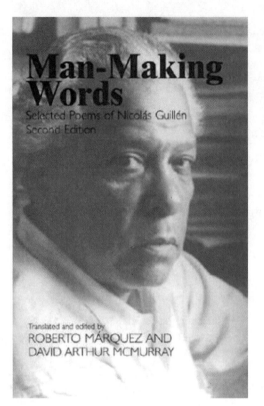

*Amherst, Mass.: University of Massachusetts Press, 1972.*

*Nacional* newspaper while attending night school to finish his education. A brief attempt at studying law in Havana failed, and he returned to Camagüey to work as a journalist. By now, he was also an accomplished and successful poet. His first poems were traditional sonnets, but he soon began to experiment with more adventurous forms of language and structure. In particular, he was keen to capture the sound and rhythm of Cuba's African-descended language and music, and in *Motivos* (1930) he produced *poemas-son* (*son*-poems), which imitated the rhythmic form of the popular musical tradition. The words were also highly political, criticising racial prejudice in Cuba and the US and attacking the basis for the economic exploitation which proliferated during the Great Depression. The next year, Guillén won a lottery prize, and this enabled him to publish *Sóngoro cosongo*, another exploration of popular music's lyrical potential. In poems like 'Song of the Bongo' and 'Rumba', he not only fused popular culture with poetic inventiveness, but also celebrated Cuba's often unsung African heritage.

During the 1930s, Guillén's political commitment became increasingly pronounced. He went to Spain during the Civil War, met Federico García Lorca and became a communist in 1937. On his return to Cuba, he worked for the newspaper *Hoy*, the mouthpiece of the Cuban Communist Party and became involved in party politics, running for mayor in his native Camagüey. He then began to travel extensively, attending writers' and peace conferences around the world throughout the 1940s. Much of that decade he spent abroad, developing his reputation throughout Latin America. In 1942 he visited Haiti, meeting his fellow communist, Jacques Roumain, for whom he later wrote an elegy. As his own communism became increasingly the centre of his life, he also began to travel widely within the Soviet bloc, visiting Moscow in 1951, and then several Eastern European countries and China. In 1954 he received the Lenin Peace Prize, in recognition of his services to international communism.

Guillén's unabashed Marxism inevitably led to trouble with the dictatorship of Fulgencio Batista, and he was twice arrested before being exiled to Paris and Buenos Aires while the Communist Party was outlawed in Cuba by Batista. This was a fertile period for his poetry, and in 1958 he published *The Dove of Popular Flight*, containing some of his most powerful and moving poems. No sooner, however, had the collection appeared than Guillén was on his way back to Cuba in the wake of Castro's successful seizure of power on January 1, 1959. On his return, Guillén's talents were pressed into service by the revolutionary government. He resumed his work as a journalist, gave public readings of his poetry and helped to establish the National Union of Cuban

Writers and Artists (UNEAC), the body intended to harness literary creativity to revolutionary objectives.

After *Tengo* came *The Great Zoo* (1967), arguably Guillén's most original work, an epic poem encompassing Caribbean history, a bestiary in the tradition of Aesop or La Fontaine and a strong dose of magical realism. This was in no sense facile propaganda, and neither was *The Daily Daily* (1972), a 64-page collage of Cuban history subverted by satire and linguistic irreverence.

For the last two decades of his life, Guillén acted as Cuba's poet laureate, at ease with the revolution and loved by all Cubans as a poet whose ideas and themes were expressed in a natural, comprehensible and lyrical voice. His fundamental concerns remained the same: the complex and violent nature of Caribbean history and the cultural melting-pot that has emerged from it. His classic *West Indies Ltd*, published in 1934, is perhaps typical of his vision of the people whom he believed could be redeemed through socialist revolution:

> This is a dark smiling people
> humble, gentle folk
> descendants of slaves
> and of that uncivil riff-raff
> of various breeds
> whom in the name of Spain
> Columbus kindly ceded to the Indies.
>
> Here are whites and blacks and Chinese and mulattoes
> They are cheap colours of course
> Since through trade and indenture
> The dyes have run and there is no stable tone.
> He who thinks otherwise should step forward and speak.

Guillén's reputation has continued to grow since his death in 1989. If he is partly remembered as a stalwart supporter of the revolution, he is also guaranteed enduring recognition by the universality of his poetic appeal and by his unique ability to create poetry out of the experiences, and often the sufferings, of his own people.

# LOUISE BENNETT

### 1919–

JAMAICA

Everyone knows people speak English in the English-speaking Caribbean. But do they? The answer, inevitably, is yes and no. Almost everybody can if they want to or have to, but many prefer to speak a variant of standard English, known variously as patois, dialect or Creole. In some circles of life – the law, academia, public life – standard English is in everyday usage, but among friends and family patois is just as, if not more, common. These languages vary from island to island, depending on the differing linguistic ingredients that have gone into them. In the ex-French-controlled territories such as Haiti or St Lucia, a French-based Creole is used. In other places like Curaçao or Suriname, Dutch plays a part in the construction of the local *papiamento*. On top of this are Spanish, the occasional word surviving from indigenous languages, a sprinkling of Hindi or Urdu and, of course, the many words brought over from different parts of Africa during the era of slavery.

Those who speak standard English fluently almost always speak patois too. But some, less educated people who are fluent in patois may be less confident in English. Standard English has always been the language of power and authority since colonial times, and English speakers have often tended to look down on patois as an inferior, uncultivated 'pidgin', something less than a proper language or a 'corruption' of a purer language. At times, this linguistic discrimination has become mixed up with racial and colour distinctions, patois being viewed as the preserve of poorer, usually darker, parts of the population. This has meant that language in the Caribbean can often be a social battleground.

In Jamaica, patois is popularly known as 'Jamaica Talk' and it is one of the richest and most expressive of local languages. But it is only relatively recently that Jamaicans became used to the idea that it might be a vehicle for literature and poetry. For centuries 'proper' literature had to be written in English, while patois was merely an oral form of communication, suitable for folk tales but little else. Now all that has changed. The advent of socially realistic fiction, of 'dub poetry' and politically committed reggae lyrics has changed the status of Jamaica Talk. At the forefront of this linguistic revolution was Louise Bennett, known simply to all Jamaicans as 'Miss Lou'.

Louise Bennett was born in Kingston on September 7, 1919 and was educated at St Simon's College and Excelsior School. From an early age she showed an unusual interest in language and performing, reciting poems and telling stories to family and friends. Her performances at church concerts and around campfires became popular events as she had a gift for coining phrases and improvising rhymes. From an early age, too, she was conscious of the social gulf between standard English and patois, noticing that dialect was almost taboo in some social circles. But among ordinary people in Kingston, the black majority, she realised that it was a vibrant form of expression, encompassing beauty, sadness and humour. English, of course, was what was taught at school, but in marketplaces, in the streets and at religious gatherings patois was the language of real communication.

The first poems Bennett wrote were in conventional English, but when she was 14, an incident on a Kingston tram bus on her way to the cinema inspired her first patois poem. When, as a portly young girl, she went to the back of the bus to find a seat, she discovered a group of market women unwilling to give up a space. Spreading themselves out over the seats, they deprived her of a place to sit but inspired the comic poem 'Spred out yuself Lisa', an imitation of the market vendors' chatter. This marked the start of Bennett's patois writing career and also reinforced her desire to perform material that she had written. Not everybody, it seems, was enthusiastic about her celebration of patois. At an

*Louise Bennett in performance*

early performance, she relates, an indignant voice was raised in protest: 'A dat yah modder sen yuh a school fa?'

After a course at the Royal Academy of Dramatic Arts in London from 1945 to 1947, Bennett worked for the BBC and in English repertory theatre for six years. She then spent two years in the US, working on the stage and on radio. When she returned to Jamaica in 1955 she was employed by the Social Welfare Commission, becoming its director in 1959. Her experiences abroad merely reinforced her belief that patois was, in many ways, a more expressive medium for many Jamaicans than standard English: 'Of course we must learn English, but I think that Jamaican people have more to say in their language than in English. It is the language of the country. It is three hundred years we have been talking it. It is not a corruption of anything.'

For the last half century 'Miss Lou' has become known to every Jamaican for her poetry. Published in book form, as albums and performed live on radio, at concerts and during the pantomime season, her poems reflect and articulate the richness of the island's cultural life. Based partly on the cadences of traditional village gossip, partly on the more abrasive sounds of urban slang, her poetry is by turns comical, indignant and sentimental. A poem like *Dutty Tough*, for instance, laments the rising cost of living and the difficulty of feeding a poor family in the face of shortages: 'Saltfish gawn up! Mackeral gawn up!/Pork an beef gawn up same way/An wan rice and butter ready/Dem jus go pon holiday!' Usually the lines are delivered as if spoken to a friend, giving the sense of a conversation – or more accurately, a monologue – held in the street. Her preferred persona is that of the big-hearted, long-suffering 'Mother Jamaica', the epitome of the island's all-surviving womanhood.

Her poems are also often ironic reflections on the events and ideas of the day. 'Back to Africa' pokes fun at the Marcus Garvey-inspired ideal of a return to a long-lost African homeland, asking Miss Matty why she should feel an ancestral link to Africa when other ancestors were English, French and Jewish. Perhaps her best-known poem is *Colonization in Reverse*, a witty commentary on the mass migration of Jamaicans to Britain in the 1950s and 1960s:

Wat a joyful news, Miss Mattie,
I feel like me heart gwine burs
Jamaica people colonizin
Englan in reverse.
By de hundred, by de tousan
From country and from town
By de ship-load, by de plane-load
Jamaica is Englan boun.

Widely honoured in her own island as well as abroad, Miss Lou has become an integral part of Jamaica's popular culture, paving the way for other, harder-hitting exponents of patois poetry. The Council of the Institute of Jamaica has conferred on the Honourable Louise Bennett-Coverley, OM, OJ, MBE, Hon DLitt, the title of the fellow of the Institute of Jamaica. Her great achievement has been to restore Jamaica's spoken language to its rightful place as a medium for poetry, both spoken and written.

S mall, arid and undeveloped, Cat Island is one of the many coral outcrops that make up the Bahamian archipelago. A place of tiny farms and rolling hills, as yet unspoilt by mass tourism, it seems a million miles away from the urban frenzy of New York or the glamour of Hollywood. Yet, this is where Sidney Poitier, arguably the greatest black actor of the modern age, spent his childhood years, and it was from here that he made his extraordinary journey towards stardom.

Poitier was actually born in Miami, as his parents had gone there to seek better medical facilities, but he was brought up on Cat Island and retains Bahamian citizenship. His father was a small farmer, coaxing tomatoes and other crops out of the island's sandy soil, and his childhood was marked by poverty and a lack of formal education. In his teens he began to behave badly, and at the age of 15 his parents decided to send him to Miami to join his older brother. There he immediately discovered the prejudice and racism that existed in many areas of American life, and he resolved not only to forge a career for himself, but to advance the cause of racial equality in any way he could. The early years in the US were tough; after an unhappy period in Miami, Poitier moved to New York, where he encountered nothing other than menial jobs and discrimination. At one point he was so penniless, he was forced to sleep on a bench in a bus station. He worked briefly as an orderly in a military veterans' hospital and gravitated towards the black centre of New York, Harlem.

## SIDNEY POITIER

1924 –

BAHAMAS

There the story might have ended, but for the fact that Poitier had decided to become an actor. Almost on an impulse he went for an audition at the American Negro Theatre, but was rejected out of hand, reportedly because his Bahamian accent was considered 'too Caribbean'. This refusal merely inspired him to work on his accent and his delivery in general, and six months later he reapplied. This time he was successful, and he was accepted by the Harlem company that also trained Harry Belafonte.

Poitier's first big break came when he was noticed during a rehearsal at the American Negro Theatre and offered a small part in a Broadway production of Aristophanes' *Lysistrata*. He was favourably mentioned in several reviews, and offers of work began to flood in. By the end of 1949, Poitier was faced with a choice between major stage roles or a début in the cinema: he chose the latter, appearing in *No Way Out* (1950), a hard-hitting melodrama in which he played the part of a black doctor treating a white bigot. Legend has it that Poitier lied to director John Mankiewicz in order to get the part, claiming that he was older than he actually was. In many ways, this first role was to become the hallmark of Poitier's distinctive style: the black character as the victim of discrimination, yet in every way superior to his white tormentors. This success was followed by a part in *Blackboard Jungle* (1955), one of the first films to explore inner-city problems of juvenile delinquency and racism.

After turning down several more roles that he judged to be stereotypical or demeaning, Poitier co-starred with Tony Curtis in Stanley Kramer's *The Defiant Ones* (1958), another moral melodrama in which he played a black convict, literally manacled to Curtis, on the run from a chain gang. This performance won him his first Academy Award nomination for best actor. Even better was to come with *Lilies of the Field* (1963), for which Poitier won an Oscar as best actor, the first time a black performer had ever achieved such a feat. The film itself was a sentimental story of an itinerant black workman, played by Poitier, who reluctantly helps a group of German nuns to build a chapel in New Mexico.

Poitier's cinematic career has spanned a wide array of roles and films, ranging from *Porgy and Bess* (1959), the 'Negro opera' made famous by Paul Robeson, to the light comedy *Uptown Saturday Night* (1974), which he also directed. But his great roles were undoubtedly in the 1960s, especially in the classic *In the Heat of the Night* (1967), in which he played the part of a black detective confronting (and eventually winning over) the bigoted sheriff in a small southern town. That performance, opposite Rod Steiger, was matched by another virtuoso appearance in *Guess Who's Coming to Dinner* (1967), Stanley Kramer's drawing-room comedy, in which a wealthy San Francisco heiress announces that she is going to marry a black man. The year 1967 saw yet another success, this time in London, as Poitier starred in *To Sir with Love*, the story of a West Indian teacher's impact on a tough school in London's East End. Here, interestingly, Poitier was encouraged to use his Caribbean accent rather than conceal it.

For many years Sidney Poitier was the best-known and most instantly recognisable black actor in the world. In a 1989 interview with the *New York Times* he admitted that his high profile and the great demands made of him were a source of considerable pressure:

> During the period when I was the only person here – no Bill Cosby, no Eddie Murphy, no Denzil Washington – I was carrying the hopes and aspirations of an entire people. I had to satisfy the action fans, the romantic fans, the intellectual fans. It was a terrific burden.

But Poitier's achievement was precisely to lead the way for later black actors, by producing performances that transcended caricature and stereotype, widening the potential for 'serious' roles. His good looks, charisma and screen presence served him well throughout his career in breaking this new ground. Intrinsically likable, Poitier always exuded a sort of moral superiority and integrity that was important in countering deep-seated prejudices. In 1968 Poitier was knighted by Queen Elizabeth II and in 2000 received the Screen Actors' Guild Lifetime Award, a prestigious token of his contribution to cinema.

In recent years Poitier's output has been less prolific, but he has shown talents beyond acting and directing. His autobiography, *This Life* (1980), is a well-written and characteristically modest account of his rise to fame. It also contains some sharp criticism of the modern-day Bahamas, in which Poitier detects too much American influence and a lack of national cultural self-awareness. Even so, he accepted the post of Bahamian Ambassador to Japan in 1997, attending a ceremony at the Imperial Palace with Emperor Akihito presiding. His attachment to the country of his birth has remained intact throughout his long career. He received the Legacy Award from the University of the West Indies in 2001 for his support of the endowment fund which provides scholarships for talented West Indians who cannot afford to attend university.

# DEREK WALCOTT

### 1930–

ST LUCIA

The Caribbean, it is fair to say, has produced many well-known novelists, but its poets are less widely celebrated. Writers of fiction such as V.S, Naipaul, George Lamming and Alejo Carpentier have won international reputations, but their poetry-writing contemporaries have, on the whole, gained less attention. This is perhaps particularly true in the English-speaking Caribbean, for Cuba has produced Nicolás Guillén, the Dominican Republic Pedro Mir, and Martinique Aimé Césaire. And yet when one looks at an anthology of English-language poetry, the roll call of first-rate poets is long and illustrious. Some, like Claude McKay or Jean Rhys, are better known as novelists; others, like Mervyn Morris and Philip Sherlock, are also known for their academic work. But names like Kamau Brathwaite, Martin Carter and E.A. Markham remind one that the English-speaking Caribbean has a living tradition of poetic excellence.

Nowhere is this more obvious than in the case of Derek Walcott. If many of his contemporaries have suffered from comparative obscurity, then he is the exception to break the rule. For in 1992, Walcott was awarded the highest accolade, the Nobel Prize for Literature, for his poetic work. It was the second time, after Sir Arthur Lewis, that the tiny island of St Lucia could claim a Nobel laureate among its people.

Derek Alton Walcott was born in Castries on January 23, 1930 into a family suffering from what he has termed 'genteel, self-denying Methodist poverty'. His father, who died when Derek and his brother Roderick were still young, was an amateur painter; his mother, a teacher, produced Shakespearean plays at the local school. Thriving within this literary and artistic household, he went to St Mary's College, Castries, and from there won a scholarship to the University College of the West Indies in Kingston, Jamaica. Walcott was a precocious poet, encouraged by his mother. By the age of 18, he had produced his first collection, *Twenty-Five Poems*, which was privately printed. He already showed a marked interest in theatre, too, writing *Henri Christophe*, a dramatic study of Haiti's deranged nineteenth-century monarch. The play was performed in 1950.

At university, Walcott studied English, French and Latin, then taught comparative literature there between 1954 and 1958 before going to study theatre in New York. He also worked as a journalist, contributing features to a Kingston newspaper. In the meantime he had established himself in Trinidad, where in 1959, he founded the Trinidad Theatre Workshop, which he directed for many years. Some of his better-known early plays, including *Dream on Monkey Mountain* (1971), received their premieres at the Theatre Workshop.

For two decades, Walcott was based mostly in Trinidad, producing an impressive corpus of poetry and drama. *In a Green Night* (1962) won him critical acclaim, with the eminent Robert Graves writing of the collection: 'Walcott handles English with a closer understanding of its inner magic than most (if not any) of his English-born contemporaries.' Further volumes appeared: *The Castaway* (1965), *The Gulf* (1973), *Sea Grapes* (1976). At the same time, Walcott was working with the Trinidad Theatre Workshop and contributing regular reviews and other pieces to the *Trinidad Guardian.*

In 1976, Walcott ended his close association with the Theatre Workshop and began teaching creative writing at various American universities. More poetry was published in the following years, including *The Fortunate Traveller* (1982) and *Midsummer* (1984). *Omeros*, perhaps his most ambitious work, appeared in 1990. An epic poem, it recasts the classical themes of Homer's *Iliad* and *Odyssey* in a Caribbean setting in which two fishermen are latter-day poetic protagonists. Post-Nobel Prize work has included a semi-autobiographical extended poem, *Tiepolo's Hound* (2000), illustrated with Walcott's own paintings, which merges the life and work of Caribbean-born Impressionist Camille Pissarro with Walcott's own responses to art and artistic traditions.

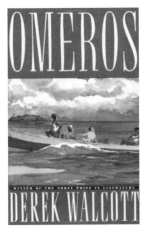

*New York: Noonday Press, 1992*

Several concerns run consistently through Walcott's extensive poetic work. One is the question of the Caribbean's complex, sometimes fractured, identity, born out of imperial rule and the horrors of the plantation system. Europe, Africa, India: all are included in his dissection of what has come together to create the Caribbean's hybrid essence. Painfully conscious of his own mixed heritage, he uses his self-definition as a 'mulatto of style' to explore the region's Creole culture. In *A Far Cry from Africa* (1962), Walcott invokes his own ancestry as a means of examining the Caribbean's wider contradictions of culture and language:

> I who am poisoned with the blood of both,
> Where shall I turn, divided to the vein?
> I who have cursed
> The drunken officer of British rule, how choose
> Between this Africa and the English tongue I love?

A preoccupation with language itself is also at the heart of Walcott's poetry. Conscious of the enormous poetic tradition of standard English, he is also deeply aware of the poetic potential within patois and especially the French-influenced Creole of his native St Lucia. Much of his poetry is written in conventional English, but he has also written widely in dialect, mixing Creole folk tradition with other, often classical, cultural allusions. The everyday language of banana farmers, fishermen or market women is, thus, woven into his poetic voice, giving his poetry an infinite range of registers and

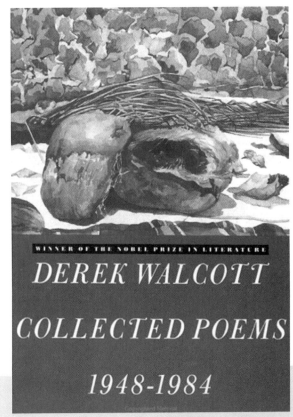

*New York: Farrar, Strauss &Giroux, 1987.*

references. Walcott's fundamental interest in speech, as reflected in his lifelong attachment to drama, finds expression also in the poetry, where echoes of calypso, song lyrics and Creole proverbs are always lying under the surface.

Walcott has been away from St Lucia for much of his adult life, but his attachment to the island remains deep and almost visceral. He has protested publicly against what he sees as the despoliation of St Lucia's spectacular natural beauty for the development of tourism, comparing the construction of a hotel between the celebrated Pitons to the building of a take-away concession at Stonehenge. In his acceptance speech at the Nobel Prize ceremony, Walcott referred to an almost primal innocence and simplicity of his island's landscapes, always threatened by the developer's bulldozer:

> How quickly it could all disappear! And how it is beginning to drive us further into where we hope are impenetrable places, green secrets at the end of bad roads, headlands where the next view is not of a hotel but of some long beach without a figure and the hanging question of some fisherman's smoke at its far end. The Caribbean is not an idyll, not to its natives.

From St Lucia's sleepy banana-growing villages to Trinidad's oil-fuelled urban frenzy, Walcott's vision of the Caribbean is all-encompassing and deeply perceptive. His poetry has succeeded in giving us an unsentimental, yet deeply affectionate, vision of Caribbean life, its landscapes, language and people. Fascinated by the region's traumatic history and resulting cultural complexity, he gives voice to the inflections and cadences of its people, celebrating both their resilient humour and the poetry inherent within their lives.

# THE VISUAL ARTS

*Michel Jean Cazabon* | *Philomé Obin* | *Edna Manley* | *Wifredo Lam*

(Trinidad and Tobago)

(Haiti)

(Jamaica)

(Cuba)

The Caribbean is by its very nature a feast for the eyes. The greens of vegetation seem more intense than elsewhere, the blues of the sea subtle and nuanced according to the time of day. Tropical flowers, such as bougainvillea, flamboyant or hibiscus, provide spectacular splashes of colour, while brightly hued birds like parrots, parakeets or hummingbirds catch the eye against a background of greenery. Humans add to this palette of colours. Many homes in the region, from the chattel houses of Barbados to the peasant *cases* of Haiti, are adorned with the brightest of greens, reds and blues, often complemented by intricate gingerbread decorations. Buses can be works of art in themselves, sporting intricate religious or natural motifs; shop signs or restaurant advertising are frequently hand painted, giving full rein to the artist's imagination. In fact, colour – and popular art – is ubiquitous in the Caribbean, reflecting an approach to life that values creativity and vitality over restraint. Celebrations, such as Carnival in Trinidad, Crop-Over in Barbados or Jonkonnu in Jamaica are further evidence of popular self-expression and an instinctive gift for design.

Unlike literature, creative arts in the Caribbean have a long history. Petroglyphs, carvings and pottery attest to the artistic talents of the region's indigenous inhabitants. The Tainos, in particular, produced a range of objects and images, many with religious significance. But colonial rule and the imposition of slavery put an effective end to the arts for several centuries until, in the nineteenth century, circumstances allowed a small revival of artistic activity. Again, its first exponents were predominantly influenced by prevailing trends in Europe and tended to conform to an imported orthodoxy. Jean-Baptiste Vermay, for instance, was responsible for several fine murals in Havana's public buildings. An early painter from Trinidad, Michel Jean Cazabon, was able to study formal technique in Europe, but his great achievement was to adapt classical convention to his tropical context, producing landscapes of great beauty and originality. A contemporary of Cazabon's, Camille Pissarro, went on to become one of the best-known of Impressionist painters. Born in the Danish-ruled island of St Thomas (now part of the US Virgin Islands), Pissarro spent his formative years in the Caribbean before establishing himself in France. He is thought to have exerted a significant influence on the Puerto Rican artist, Francisco Manuel Oller, who combined Impressionist technique with a series of moving anti-slavery subjects in the 1860s.

Another Caribbean-born artist who went abroad to make his name was John James Audubon, who was born in Les Cayes, Haiti, in 1785, the illegitimate son of a French naval officer and a local woman. He became the internationally known author of *Birds of America*, illustrated by him with 400 hand-tinted life-size plates. His name lives on in the National Audubon Society, the US organisation concerned with preserving bird life.

Caribbean art really began to make an impact internationally from the 1940s onwards. First came the discovery of the Haitian 'naïve' painters such as Hector Hyppolite, Philomé Obin and Préfète Duffaut. Soon their canvases were fetching thousands of dollars on the American market, and hundreds more artists scrambled to join the boom, rapidly devaluing Haitian art's reputation. At the same time, the Cuban artist Wifredo Lam, inspired by Picasso's Cubism, the iconoclastic outlook of surrealism and the ancestral symbolism of Afro-Cuba, began his powerful visual evocations of a mysterious spiritual world. Other artists, in the Dominican Republic, Puerto Rico and the French islands, also began to merge abstract techniques with imagery specific to the Caribbean: landscapes, colour, religious motifs. In Jamaica, the barber-painter, John Dunkley, demonstrated an entirely self-taught, intuitive grasp of colour and symbolism, which brought him considerable but posthumous fame.

The arrival of tourism did much to encourage artistic output from the 1950s onwards, but the urge to produce affordable souvenirs often ran counter to the requirements of quality control. Paintings and sculptures were literally mass-produced, many poor imitations of early Haitian art. Even so, some artists continued to create work of a non-commercial and original nature. Guyana's Aubrey Williams, for example, worked in the field of abstract impressionism, inspired by the traditional gestural symbolism of Guyana's Amerindian population.

Under the aegis of Edna Manley, the British-born wife of Norman Manley, the artistic world in Jamaica underwent something of a revolution. Driven by the prevailing mood of nationalism and experimentation, she and a circle of followers attacked the conservative colonial establishment within the world of arts. Surrounded by painters such as Albert Huie and sculptors like Alvin Marriott, Edna Manley played a pivotal role in changing attitudes and building the infrastructure for a dynamic national arts movement. Today, Kingston's National Gallery testifies to the vitality of that movement, featuring work by artists such as Cecil Baugh, Barrington Watson and Colin Garland. Manley's own sculptures are also on display.

There is also a good deal of vitality in the contemporary arts scene in other Caribbean countries. Haiti is once again a source of originality, with painters like Edouard Duval-Carrié and metal sculptors such as Serge Jolimeau commanding high prices for their work. Cuba and the Dominican Republic are also producing interesting painting, exhibited in commercial art galleries and national institutions. And across the Caribbean, countless artists and sculptors are creating work of lasting value out of wood, clay and metal, much of it destined for European and North American art lovers.

# MICHEL JEAN CAZABON
## 1813–1888

TRINIDAD AND TOBAGO

Almost any tourist shop on any Caribbean island will have a stock of locally produced paintings. Often gaudily bright and 'naïve' in style, they are typically meant to recreate the vibrancy of a Caribbean landscape or market scene. This sort of painting is what many associate with the region. Moreover, it is generally assumed that the islands have produced significant painters only within the last century, that an indigenous art tradition began with the 'discovery' of Haitian primitive painters in the 1940s. The work of Michel Jean Cazabon, little known for many years after his death, reveals that the Caribbean, far from being an artistic desert in the nineteenth century, produced at least one world-class watercolourist who adopted and perfected the techniques in vogue in Europe at the time.

Cazabon's parents, François and Rose, emigrated to Trinidad from Martinique in about 1790. It was a period of political tumult in the French islands in the wake of revolution in Paris and they opted for the security of British-owned Trinidad. As 'free coloureds' they were of mixed race, but had never been slaves. Indeed, they were prosperous enough to acquire Corynth Estate at North Naparima, one of the many sugar plantations around the southern town of San Fernando. It was there that Michel Jean, their fourth child, was born on September 20, 1813.

Michel Jean's parents were anxious that he should have a formal European education, so in 1826 they dispatched him on a ship to England, where he had a place at St Edmund's College at Ware in Hertfordshire. The following year he took his first drawing lesson, and although there is no record of how his teacher responded, we must assume it was positively. After four years of English boarding school, he returned to Trinidad. Some time later he moved with his mother to Port of Spain, but in 1837, he set off for Europe once more, this time for Paris. There he studied at the École des Beaux-Arts under the influential artist and professor Paul Delaroche, a painter who specialised in popular and often sentimental historical landscapes. Understandably, his own style was heavily influenced by Delaroche's teaching and within two years he had become skilled enough to exhibit his own work at the Salon du Louvre, one of the most prestigious annual exhibitions to be held in Paris. That year he sold a painting, *The Assumption of the Virgin*, to the French government for 600 francs. Cazabon was launched on a career as a professional artist, supported by his family's background wealth.

For the next decade, Cazabon travelled restlessly between Paris, Italy and Trinidad. He studied further in Italy in 1841 and then returned to Paris, where he met and married Louise Rosalie Trolard; the next year his daughter Rose was born. Exhibiting each year at the Salon du Louvre, he was gradually building up a reputation as a fine landscape artist, and the prices his pictures fetched rose accordingly. After a son, Louis Michel, was born in 1845, Cazabon returned to Trinidad, leaving his family behind in Paris. This was probably one of the most creative periods in his life.

Cazabon's great achievement was to transplant the contemporary landscape techniques of Europe into the tropical setting of his native Trinidad. He was particularly interested in scenes that would convey the exotic wilderness of the island, but also specialised in coastal scenes, contrasting the varying blues of the Caribbean Sea with the lush vegetation of the hillsides running down towards the water. Perhaps his most celebrated painting is *Bamboos at Maqueripe*, in which the huge stems of the bamboo plants rise up majestically to frame a strolling couple. The overall impression is of a bucolic, but distinctly exotic, mixture of nature and human interest.

Cazabon's favourite area in Trinidad was the north-west peninsula around Chaguaramas. There he painted the many small islands of Monos, Huevos and Chacachacare as well as the Dragon's Mouth straits. These paintings record the spectacular natural beauty of Trinidad's north coast – a beauty that is largely intact to this day. Cazabon also recorded events of historical interest; his *The Landing of the Atlantic Cable at Macqueripe* documents the arrival of the first transatlantic telegraph cable in Trinidad. He was fascinated by different perspectives and by the different quality of light produced by changing weather conditions. Few of his paintings show the unrealistic clear blue sky of the modern-day tourist brochure, and instead he reproduced intricate cloud formations and hazy horizons.

After a brief return to Paris in 1851 and the birth of his third child there the following year, Cazabon finally returned to Trinidad, from where he subsequently began to travel widely in the Caribbean. Following the death of his father, the sale of a sugar plantation seems to have secured his financial position, and he visited Martinique, Grenada and British Guiana, where he produced further watercolours and oil landscapes. By now his work was appreciated by wealthy collectors, and he received commissions to paint particular paintings or series of paintings. Lord Harris,

*Old Negroes, French in Gala Dress*

the Governor of Trinidad between 1846 and 1854, commissioned Cazabon to produce no fewer than 32 watercolours and six oil paintings, depicting a wide range of Trinidadian views and events. This work took Cazabon six years to complete; today the collection can be seen in its entirety in Belmont House, near Faversham, Kent, the house belonging to the Harris family.

In 1862 Cazabon, who remained attached to French and French Creole culture throughout his life, moved to Martinique, where he remained for eight years. He painted and exhibited there before returning once more to Trinidad. In later years he was much less prolific than in the 1840s and 1850s, but he continued to publish work in lithographic collections. As late as 1886, the year after the death of his wife, he exhibited 16 watercolours and 12 pen and ink drawings at the Colonial and Indian Exhibition in London. The following year, on November 20, Cazabon died. He was buried with no great ceremony in Port of Spain the following day.

Cazabon was little known during his own lifetime, especially in later years, and it took many years for his originality and vision to become appreciated in the Caribbean. Today, however, he is honoured as one of Trinidad and Tobago's national heroes, and in 1997, his work featured prominently in an exhibition of Trinidadian painting, old and new, in London. Normally many of his paintings are on show in Port of Spain's National Museum and Art Gallery. After a long period of neglect, Cazabon's painting is today recognised as a landmark in the development of Caribbean art, and he is remembered as one of the few black artists of the nineteenth century to produce work of internationally acclaimed quality.

*Wedding of Lord Harris. Trinity Church, 1850, Port-of-Spain*

# PHILOMÉ OBIN

## 1891–1986

HAITI

Perhaps more than any other Caribbean country, Haiti is a land inhabited by ghosts and spirits. Some are the deities worshipped in *vodou* ceremonies: Erzulie, the goddess of love, or Dambala, the life force. These are an amalgam of traditional African gods and the saints of the Catholic Church, the result of a syncretic mixing of faiths and ceremonies. *Vodou* has been much maligned and distorted by the outside world since African slaves transported ancestral beliefs with them to the colonial plantations of Saint Domingue. Caricatured as an evil form of witchcraft, the spirituality of Haitian folk religion has often been reduced to a handful of Hollywood zombie clichés.

But other ghosts make their presence felt in Haiti. These are the spectres of the country's history, the individuals who are remembered today as forging the nation's past. Historic figures such as Toussaint L'Ouverture, Jean-Jacques Dessalines and even 'Papa Doc' Duvalier are ever-present in popular culture, in *vodou* ceremonies, in story telling, in art. And art is everywhere in Haiti. Walls in towns and cities boast colourful murals, the *tap-taps* (buses) that weave through the crowded streets are kaleidoscopic displays of colour and design, while thousands of painters and sculptors produce work that has become internationally famous.

The first Haitian art 'boom' occurred in the 1940s, when an American would-be painter, DeWitt Peters, went to Haiti as a volunteer English teacher. There he was bowled over by what he saw as the 'self-taught and instinctive' artists he met. In 1944, he was behind the opening of the Centre d'Art in Port-au-Prince, a gallery and training facility designed to publicise and encourage this prodigious talent. One of the first Haitian 'primitives' to be brought to prominence was Hector Hyppolite, a *vodou* priest and ex-house painter, whose religious imagery and sense of the mysterious won immediate admiration from critics and collectors. So impoverished was Hyppolite that he used chicken feathers rather than paint brushes, but in the last three years of his life he produced some 250 paintings. Hyppolite died in 1948.

Born three years before Hyppolite in 1891, was another of Haiti's best-known 'naïve' painters, Philomé Obin. He originated from Bas Limbé, near the northern city of Cap-Haïtien, and relatively little is known about his early life other than he showed a conspicuous gift for painting. The year in which the Centre d'Art was opened he sent one of his paintings – a homage to US President Roosevelt, who had ended the American Occupation of Haiti in 1934. DeWitt Peters received the painting in the post, liked it and sent Obin an encouraging letter. Obin replied at once, stating that he

*Lawyer and Doctor Rosalvo Bobo, Supreme Leader of the Revolution of 1915, his Cabinet and Some Members of his Staff Watch the Arrival of the Wounded, 1956*

wished to become the historian of his nation in paint. As the relationship between the painter and the Centre d'Art developed, he was employed to build a branch of the institution in Cap-Haïtien, thereby assisting artists from the north of the country.

Obin's passion was the reconstruction through the visual medium of Haiti's turbulent history. One of his most famous paintings was *The Funeral of Charlemagne Péralte* (1946), a vastly ambitious depiction of the crowds who attended the funeral of the heroic guerrilla fighter, killed by the occupying American troops in 1918. The art critic Seldon Rodman estimated that there were no fewer than 750 individual portraits of those in attendance, while the painting was given a quasi-religious meaning by the image of Péralte as a crucified martyr and his mother, standing like Mary, at the foot of the cross. The painting thus commemorated one of the pantheon of Haitian national heroes, conferring on Péralte a sort of symbolic sanctity.

In 1951, Obin was persuaded to travel to Port-au-Prince to contribute to an extraordinary experiment in public art. Under the guidance of Bishop Alfred Voegli (later to fall foul of the Duvalier dictatorship), the Episcopalian Holy Trinity Cathedral commissioned a series of religious murals, intended to express the Christian faith of the Haitian people in their own images. It was a controversial initiative, not least because many of the painters involved were either Catholics or associated with *vodou*. Nor did the conservative hierarchy of the Roman Catholic Church approve, for many believed that the representation of biblical scenes in a Haitian context came close to blasphemy.

Obin's two major contributions to the Cathedral can still be viewed today. A *Crucifixion* on the central wall of the apse depicts Christ on the cross, surrounded by human figures modelled on the population of Cap-Haïtien, many in their Sunday best, as if unaware of the importance of the scene they are witnessing. *The Last Supper* shows a pale-skinned Christ surrounded by disciples of differing complexions, some in modern dress and most deliberately defying conventional rules of scale and perspective. Although age has faded the murals somewhat, they maintain their ability to surprise through the boldness of their execution and their eye-catching composition.

Always keen to recreate moments of Haitian history, Obin was first and foremost a communicator. There is nothing obscure about his painting, and in most cases he included a written caption on his paintings, explaining the scene to those who might be unfamiliar with a particular episode. His form of 'primitivism' involved an intentional emphasis on the old-fashioned or anachronistic. As Sheldon Williams observed:

> Obin's models are antique. Even when he is painting a 'contemporary' scene the inescapable flavour of 'yesterday' is present. The people in his pictures hold themselves stiffly as if they are posing for some Caribbean Daguerre. The old houses look too new – a flash-back to a previous century. Equipages replace the motorcar . . . Philomé Obin is the recognisable naïve painter. As a Haitian artist, he can be regarded as a natural parallel to Douanier Rousseau in France.

Like Rousseau, Obin creates a sense of the bizarre, of the unexpected, by the unlikely rearrangement of detail and by curious touches of surrealism. His painting of Dessalines riding to his quarters at Crête-à-Pierrot, shows the independence fighter and his officers passing through what looks like a formal garden, with trees symmetrically lining the road. The famous *Toussaint L'Ouverture and the French Staff* depicts Toussaint's arrest, but its drama is somehow subverted by the fact that the cluster of French soldiers, with one exception, sport identical black moustaches and carry absurdly thin, rapier-like swords.

Obin has been categorised along with Hector Hyppolite as a founding father of Haitian art. In fact, the two were very different; Obin was a much slower, less prolific artist than his contemporary. He was also a staunch Protestant, vehemently hostile to *vodou*, who sang hymns and prayed as he painted. In style and theme, too, the painters were entirely distinctive, Obin's historical interests were very far apart from Hyppolite's religious symbolism.

Apart from his own work, Obin's main contribution to Haitian art was his patronage of the Cap-Haïtien painting community, which included many of his own relatives such as Antoine and Sénèque Obin. He died on June 8, 1986, just four months after Jean-Claude 'Baby Doc' Duvalier fled Haiti in the face of a popular uprising. It was a moment celebrated by hundreds of Haiti's painters, all of whom owe much to Obin and his artistic genius.

*Four Innocent Wretches Executed*

# EDNA MANLEY

### 1900–1987

JAMAICA

Outside the reconstructed Georgian court house at Morant Bay, Jamaica, stands an imposing statue of Paul Bogle. Holding a machete that points downwards and with a grimly resolute face, the statue represents the leader of the so-called Morant Bay Rebellion of 1865, the Baptist deacon and champion of the poor. Bogle was held responsible for the brief but bloody uprising that shook colonial Jamaica when a band of landless and desperate rural labourers marched on Morant Bay. Some whites were killed and the court house was burned down. The retribution meted out by the authorities was savage. A hundred or more were hanged, including Bogle, whose body swung from the centre arch of the gutted court house. In 1965, builders discovered 79 skeletons in the vicinity of the building.

The statue says much about Jamaican history, about its deep currents of rebellion and reprisal, struggle and martyrdom. Bogle is now a national hero, remembered for his advocacy on behalf of the poor, and the statue successfully evokes his strength of purpose and courage. It is the work of Edna Manley, wife of Norman Manley, viewed by many as the founding father of modern Jamaica and architect of its most successful political party. The Manley family, especially Norman and his son Michael, is of course best known for its political legacy to the nation, but Edna Manley also had a vital role to play in the creation of an independent and vibrant artistic culture in the island.

Born Edna Swithenbank on March 1, 1900, she was the daughter of a Methodist minister and his Jamaican-born wife. Although white-skinned, she remained proud of her Jamaican ancestry throughout her life. After a childhood and adolescence in Hampshire and Cornwall (where she discovered an abiding fascination with the sea and a love of horse-riding), Edna went to study sculpture in London, attending the Regent Street Polytechnic, the Royal Academy and St Martin's School of Art.

When the First World War ended, her cousin, Norman Manley returned from the battlefields of Flanders to continue his legal studies in London. It was then that he met and resolved to marry her. They were married in 1921 and the following year Edna Manley accompanied her husband back to Jamaica, where he intended to establish himself as a lawyer. She wished to maintain an independent career as an artist and sculptress and she produced a number of sculptures in the 1920s and early 1930s which reflected current trends in British theory and practice. To begin with, she also returned to London to continue her studies, specialising in wood carving. The revolutionary aesthetics of Vorticism, associated with the modernist rejection of traditional classical sculpture, seem to have influenced her, and critics have detected the particular influence of Jacob Epstein.

Her first real success as an artist came in 1929, when she had a one-woman exhibition in London. Her wood carvings, in particular, were the subject of very favourable critical attention, and she was elected to the London Group, a prestigious collective of avant-garde artists.

Yet what set Manley apart from her British contemporaries was her growing involvement in the political and social ferment of her adopted Jamaica. In the 1930s a wave of social unrest, not unlike Bogle's ill-fated rebellion, swept through the Caribbean, and from it emerged the first political parties and trade unions that would take the British colonies towards independence. Norman Manley, like his cousin Alexander Bustamante, was at the centre of these developments. As the momentum of social change intensified, so Edna Manley's work began to reflect its tumultuous atmosphere. Her famous piece *Negro Aroused* (1935) is a dramatic depiction of an individual straining upwards against some form of constriction or oppression. Allegorically, it reflects the aspirations and struggles of Jamaica's black majority – the same people who were becoming attracted to the change promised by Norman Manley and his People's National Party.

*Edna Manley at work*

In the context of colonial Jamaica, art was very much the preserve of a privileged few and tended to look towards the 'mother country' for inspiration. Jamaica's African roots were often dismissed or ignored, while the education system perpetuated British themes and concepts in all areas of self-expression. Edna Manley was opposed to this state of affairs and gradually began to nurture what she saw as a truly indigenous art movement. She began to organise art classes at the Institute of Jamaica and encouraged several promising young artists and writers who formed a circle associated with her. Among her protégés, dubbed the *Focus* group after an arts magazine edited by Manley from 1943 onwards, were the painter, Albert Huie, the sculptor, Alvin Marriott, and the novelist and painter, Roger Mais. Meeting together to discuss politics as well artistic questions, Manley's circle was instrumental in challenging the conservatism of the Institute of Jamaica. Manley and other volunteers began to expand their teaching, and this developed into more formal training until in 1950, the Jamaica School of Art was finally established.

Edna Manley's contribution to the evolution of an authentic Jamaican arts movement was immense. Today her name is remembered in the Edna Manley College

*Negro Aroused,*
*1935*

of the Visual and Performing Arts, which encompasses schools of art, music, dance and drama.

The explicit political iconography of Manley's 1930s work gradually gave way to a more abstract, symbolic period in the 1940s, with carvings like *Horse of the Morning* (1943) and *Land* (1945), in which the forms are more subtle and elusive. The following decade saw another shift in emphasis, as Norman Manley became chief minister in 1955 and political and social obligations mounted up for his wife. Nevertheless, among constant meetings and receptions, she found time to escape to her studio to produce fine work such as the *Crucifix* (1950) for All Saints Church, Kingston, and *He Cometh Forth* (1962), a piece commissioned to commemorate Jamaican independence. Throughout this period, Edna Manley had to share her husband's frustrations and disappointments over the collapse of the West Indies Federation and the electoral success of his opponent, Bustamante. In the Manley family she was the intuitive, unpredictable foil to the rational, dependable figure of her husband.

When Norman Manley died in 1969, Edna created a final series of wooden carvings related to his death and her grief. She then turned to more abstract subjects in various materials, including clay, before in her final years reverting to painting. Her granddaughter Rachel describes one of her last sculptures, *Ghetto Mother:*

A woman protecting her terrified children, who were huddled around her. Two outstretched arms, all she had to protect them from the guns of the ghetto and the politics of Jamaica's sons . . . Even in bronze I can still see the clay, the tops of her fingers forever inverted in its mass, each hollowed print a mouth bearing its worn-out cry to the mob beyond, to the chaos that betrayed the ghetto mother, to the past, to the future, each a sound in the wounds of the clay, a sound from the failing lungs of my withering grandmother.

*The Beadseller, bronze, 1922*

His paintings are unmistakable. Vast figures, part human, part animal, part abstraction, loom up against imprecise, suggestive backgrounds, textured and richly coloured. Strange objects, perhaps serving some ceremonial or religious purpose, also occupy the canvases, or luxuriant vegetation, both seductive and threatening. These are the dream-like paintings of Wifredo Lam, the Cuban-born painter who was a friend of Picasso and the celebrated French surrealist, André Breton. Lam has been described as a Caribbean surrealist, as an artist who adapted the revolutionary principles of surrealism within a Cuban context. But it is probably fairer to say that he created something more original than a variant on European surrealism, that his work was much more a product of his original environment and a life-long interest in Cuba's African heritage.

# WIFREDO LAM
## 1902–1982
CUBA

Wifredo Oscar de la Concepción Lam y Castilla was born on December 8, 1902 in Sagua La Grande, in the north coast area of Villa Clara province. His father, Lam Yam, was a Chinese-born shopkeeper who had come to Cuba via San Francisco. His mother, of mixed African origins, had been a slave before the abolition of slavery in Cuba in 1886. The last of nine children and the only boy, Wifredo was deeply influenced by his parents and, in particular, by their religious beliefs. Lam Yam practised Confucianism, including ritual sacrifices to ancestors, while his mother was a devout Catholic. Perhaps most influential, however, was his godmother, Mantonica Wilson, who was a priestess in the Santería religion. From an early age, then, Lam was exposed to a potent mix of religious faiths and rituals, producing in him an inexhaustible interest in sacred symbolism and magic.

Lam Yam's business was successful enough for the family to send Wifredo to Havana to study law. At the age of 14 he moved to the capital, but already he was more interested in painting than in legal training. When he was 12 he had already been producing competent sketches and oil paintings of local scenes, and in Havana he spent more time sketching plants and trees in the Botanical Gardens than studying. To the disappointment of his parents, Lam eventually abandoned law and studied art at the San Alejandro Academy, where he remained for five years. There he reportedly disliked the constraints of formal teaching and preferred to paint scenes and people in the streets of Havana.

In 1923 Lam left Cuba for Spain, where he believed he would come into contact with a wider range of artistic influences. He studied under the traditionalist Fernando Álvarez de Sotomayor, curator at the Prado Museum, but in the evenings he worked in studios where younger avant-garde painters gathered. It was a period of intense learning; at the Prado he admired the grotesque painting of Hieronymus Bosch and Brueghel, elsewhere he became acquainted with the exoticism of Paul Gauguin and

*La Silla (The Chair), 1943.*

the Impressionism of Cézanne. It was also a period of tragedy. In 1931, his Spanish wife, Eva Piriz, and his infant son both died of tuberculosis.

Politics also became important to Lam, as Spain slid into civil war after Franco's military coup against the Republican government. His personal tragedy also fuelled his hatred of poverty and inequality, and he was drawn to the Left. He fought against Franco's Fascist-supported troops in the defence of Madrid, but was on the losing side, and in 1938 he joined the Republican exodus to Paris. There he had a letter of introduction to Pablo Picasso, himself a supporter of the Republican cause who in 1936 had painted the famous denunciation of Franco's militarism, *Guernica*.

Inspired by Picasso, Lam produced a series of gouache works, featuring strange, hieratic figures that seemed to owe much to the African sculpture in vogue in Paris at the time. These works are strongly reminiscent of Picasso's Cubist period, depicting hybrid forms and a strong element of the fantastic. He also met a range of influential writers and artists, all of whom were intent on pushing back the boundaries of conventional aesthetics. Chief among these was André Breton, the charismatic leader of the surrealist movement, who mixed revolutionary politics with a radical rejection of traditional literature and a quest for new forms of self-expression. In 1940, as the Germans advanced on Paris, Lam, Breton and many other intellectuals fled to the relative safety of Marseille before taking a ship to the French Caribbean colony of Martinique.

Seven months later, in 1942, Lam was back in Cuba, and it was at this point that all the influences he had absorbed – from his childhood to his days in Paris – seemed to come together. His most famous work, *The Jungle* (1943), reveals these manifold impressions, as a surrealist juxtaposition of clashing images combines with the magical symbolism of Afro-Cuban folk culture. Against a background of sharp, sugarcane-like foliage that becomes indistinguishable from the limbs of the figures in the foreground, four large masks, both exotic and terrifying, stare out of the picture. In its absolute rejection of conventional perspective and subject matter, the painting clearly owes much to both Picasso and surrealism. But in its evocation of religious or spiritual mystery, strongly coloured by African associations, it is possible to see recollections of Lam's childhood experience of popular Cuban religion. In a painting like *Femme Cheval* (*Horse Woman*, 1960), the religious allusion is just as explicit, the bizarre horse-woman hybrid referring to the moment in Santería ceremonies when the believer is 'ridden' or temporarily possessed by spirits. A visit to Haiti in 1946, in the company of Breton, increased Lam's fascination for Afro-Caribbean religious ceremony, notably *vodou* or voodoo.

With the war in Europe over, Lam returned to Paris in 1946 by way of New York. For a while he moved between Paris, New York and Havana, but from 1952 was mostly in the French capital. As his fame increased, his work was exhibited internationally, earning high prices and winning many prizes. He also experimented in making ceramics and sculptures, the latter cast in metal and similar in form to the figures in his paintings.

The Cuban revolution of 1959 occurred while Lam was abroad and although he never publicly criticised Fidel Castro or his regime's censorship of 'counter-revolutionary' art, he spent little time in Havana until 1978, when illness drove him to seek treatment in Cuba. It is said that Castro asked him to become minister of culture in 1962 but that Lam politely declined, saying that he was an artist, not a politician. In any case, he remained well-disposed towards the revolution, helping to win the support of artists and intellectuals in Paris and elsewhere. It was, however, in Paris that Lam died on September 11, 1982, an internationally recognised figure in the world of contemporary art.

Today, a Wifredo Lam Centre exists in Havana, dedicated to his memory and intended to encourage other Cuban painters. As Cuban art becomes increasingly valuable, so do the many canvases attributed to Lam, some of which have commanded prices in excess of half a million dollars. They continue to attract interest and admiration for the striking originality of their composition and for the way in which Lam merged the avant-garde techniques of European modernism with the ancestral images of his native Cuba.

# CARIBBEAN SOUNDS

**Celia Cruz**

(Cuba)

**Mighty Sparrow**

(Grenada)

**Bob Marley**

(Jamaica)

**Juan Luis Guerra**

(Dominican Republic)

**Kassav**

(Guadeloupe)

Forget bananas and bauxite. Forget sugarcane and rum. The most significant exports from the Caribbean in the last century (not counting its people) have been its musical sounds. The list is endless: bachata, calypso, dub; reggae, salsa, son; merengue, soca, zouk. From almost every island, regardless of size, have emerged musicians of world stature whose popularity and influence stretch far beyond the Caribbean itself. Some islands have become associated with a particular musical form. People tend to associate Jamaica with reggae, Trinidad with calypso, or Cuba with salsa. Yet although these broad categorisations hold some truth, there is also a constant process of inter-island cross-pollination, of evolving musical styles as new influences are accepted and adapted. Reggae booms out of beachside bars in Barbados, Martinican zouk blares out of minibuses in Dominica or St Lucia, Dominican bachata echoes wistfully through the *barrios* of Puerto Rico.

Music in the Caribbean has always been a blend of influences, a mix of styles. European colonists brought with them the classical and popular forms of their age, together with contemporary instruments, while from Africa arrived a rich tradition of percussion-driven sound. Later, indentured labourers from India came accompanied by their *tassa* drums and *dantal* metal rods, adding to the musical cocktail. The proximity of the US added further ingredients, not least jazz, rock 'n' roll, gospel and soul music. While some musical forms remained more or less unadulterated, such as those designed to maintain the identity of African secret societies, most were vulnerable to creative contagion from other traditions.

Then there has been the inventiveness of Caribbean people themselves. Nobody is quite sure who it was who discovered that an empty oil drum could be transformed into a melodious musical instrument, but the discovery in the late 1930s gave birth to one of the region's most evocative sounds – steelband. Local musicians have always been creative in their experimentation with the latest technological possibilities or with fusing a new style with an established form. Trinidad's chutney-soca is a case in point, combining Hindi lyrics and the traditional Indian *dholak* with the upbeat calypso-derived dance rhythm of soca.

Caribbean music is first and foremost pleasure, entertainment, escapism. But its roots lie deep in the region's history of exploitation and resistance and its function has often been subversive. During the plantation era, masters and overseers allowed their slaves to enjoy music as a sort of social safety valve, and the slaves took full advantage of this one crumb of freedom, using music as a vehicle for collective identity and for mocking their oppressors. Out of this counter-culture evolved the beginnings of forms like calypso, where African call-and-response structures became mixed with European ballads and other imported types of music to create a genre that is both satirical and harmonious, bitter and joyful. Try as they might, the colonial authorities could never stamp out this disrespectful music. In the latter part of the twentieth century, calypsonians such as the Mighty Sparrow, Chalkdust and the late lamented Lord Kitchener took the form to its highest levels of creativity and social commentary.

Reggae music, perhaps the best-known of the Caribbean's musical exports, was also born out of social unrest and protest. Its birthplace was the slums of West Kingston, where poverty and criminality were matched by the astounding musical talent of individuals such as Bob Marley, Jimmy Cliff and Toots Hibbert. Mutating from the earlier popular forms of ska and rock steady, reggae reached its international peak in the 1970s and 1980s when downtown Kingston was the scene of escalating political violence. Since the death of Marley, reggae has continued to evolve, moving away from the 'conscious', Rastafari-influenced lyrics of the 1980s to a brash, often controversial, expression of ghetto life and sexuality in dancehall music.

The sounds of the Hispanic Caribbean, most recently salsa, have also taken the world by storm. Here again, African rhythms have married with European instrumentation to produce the Latin big band sound. From Cuba, Puerto Rico and the Dominican Republic have come a rich succession of dance-oriented bands and singers, of whom the late Celia Cruz is perhaps one of the most celebrated. In the 1950s, cha-cha-cha enjoyed a brief international boom as the music that epitomised the hedonism of Havana's pre-revolutionary nightclubs. Today it is salsa that is the craze in clubs throughout Europe and North America, while films such as *Buena Vista Social Club* have revealed to an international audience the wealth of Cuba's musical heritage.

The sheer variety of Caribbean music becomes increasingly apparent as new forms continue to achieve international prominence. Haiti's rock-influenced *rasin* (roots) music has grown in strength and popularity since the overthrow of the Duvalier dictatorship in 1986, while in the neighbouring Dominican Republic, Juan Luis Guerra, has revitalised traditional folk forms such as bachata by incorporating them into lushly produced commercial recordings. And so Caribbean music, in its bewildering diversity, continues to develop and change, while all the time remaining the heartbeat of the region.

# CELIA CRUZ

### 1924–2003
#### CUBA

The explosion of salsa music's popularity was one of the most surprising cultural phenomena of the 1990s. From Europe to North America – and, of course, including the Spanish-speaking Caribbean and Latin America – young people discovered, and danced to, a highly rhythmic big band sound, in which percussion instruments such as bongos and timbales form the background to a punchy brass section. The salsa trend became so fashionable that dance classes started up in almost every city, teaching people how to move their feet and hips to this most Latin of rhythms.

Salsa means 'sauce', the hot, piquant sauce that brings zest to Hispanic cooking. Its roots are deep and varied, beginning with the African rhythms imported during the time of slavery into the Americas, but mixed with European and American influences such as jazz and rock'n'roll. Like most Creole cultural forms, it is a hybrid cocktail of elements, but its overall flavour is strongly Spanish. Several countries claim to be the heartland of salsa: Venezuela, Colombia, Panama, the Dominican Republic and Puerto Rico have all produced salsa artists of world stature, but the island that has the firmest claim to inventing, and perfecting, the form is Cuba. From the *son* of the 1920s, through mambo, cha-cha-cha and rumba, Cuba has produced an endless stream of innovative dance forms, culminating in present-day salsa, described as 'the child of *son*.' But salsa is also the product of migration and exile, of inner-city *barrios* in New York and other US cities. This, where some of the best clubs and recording studios are to be found.

Most Latin countries, as well as New York's Barrio Latino, can boast their salsa superstar: Ruben Bladés from Panama, Oscar D'León from Venezuela, Ray Barreto from Puerto Rico. But the title of 'Queen of Salsa' undisputedly belongs to Celia Cruz, the Cuban-born singer who was described by the *New York Times* as 'one of the world's great singers'.

Celia Cruz, we know, was born on October 21, although she always chose to keep the year of her birth a secret. Estimates range from 1916 to 1929, but biographers think that 1924 is the likeliest contender. In any case, she was born one of 14 children in Barrio Santra Suarez, a small town near Havana. As a child she showed unusual musical promise, singing her brothers and sisters to sleep and entertaining friends and neighbours with her distinctive voice. Her parents wanted Celia to be a teacher and she started studying towards that goal, but a cousin encouraged her to develop her vocal skills, and she was persuaded to sing a tango on a local radio station. She won a prize and her career was launched.

In the 1930s and 1940s, during her childhood and adolescence, Cuba was alive with music. Its night life was legendary and there was already a powerful recording industry, with a flourishing network of radio stations. The young Celia Cruz was exposed to a wide range of musical influences, including *son* and jazz, and in 1947 she decided, against her parents' advice, to study at Havana's Conservatory of Music. Although she learned a great deal about musical theory at the Conservatory, she claims to have ignored voice training, as she felt that formal instruction was unnecessary for a singer who valued authenticity over taught technique.

Cruz's first performances were mostly comprised of the slower forms of Afro-Cuban protest song, but she soon shifted to the more upbeat *guaracha* style, with its strong elements of humour and satire. In 1950, she was hired as lead singer for Cuba's top dance band, La Sonora Matancera. It was an extraordinary stroke of luck for the inexperienced Cruz and she immediately began recording and performing for enormous audiences across Latin America. During the 1950s, Cuban music won even greater recognition, due to her band as well as such stars as Tito Puente, Pérez Prado and Desi Arnaz. La Sonora Matancera toured and recorded tirelessly.

*Celia Cruz performing*

The band was touring Mexico when Fidel Castro's revolution toppled the dictatorial regime of Fulgencio Batista in late 1958. When the revolutionary forces entered Havana, the band decided not to return to Cuba and stayed in Mexico before settling more permanently in New York. According to Cruz, 'Castro never forgave me' for what he may have seen as an act of hostility on her part. Subsequently, relations between the singer and the regime in Havana were unfriendly. Cruz claimed that she was not allowed to return to the island to visit her ageing parents. The Cuban government, on the other hand, did not fail to notice a strong element of criticism in her songs, tinged with nostalgia for a lost homeland.

Celia Cruz remained with La Sonora Matancera until 1965, when she joined Tito Puente's specially recruited band. Together they recorded eight albums, but without huge success. Gradually, however, the new vogue for salsa music was beginning to take off in New York. 'Salsa was a name given to Cuban music in the '60s in New York', she recalled. 'At that time, a lot of Cuban orchestras were playing, and they gave it that name as a kind of commercial name. In general, it's called Cuban music, but there were different rhythms, like the rumba, guaguanco, cha-cha-cha, son. Today all those rhythms together are called salsa.'

Riding the tide of the initial salsa vogue, Cruz signed to Yaya Records, the sister label of Fania, the leader in salsa production and so began a long succession of records and tours. After recording with fellow *salseros* like D'León and the Puerto Rican Héctor 'Tito' Rodríguez, she achieved a first gold album in the early 1970s with *Celia and Johnny*, recorded with the flute-playing Johnny Pacheco, vice-president of the Fania label. From there it was a logical move to join the Fania Allstars, perhaps the most talented and successful of all salsa bands. She continued recording and performing throughout the 1980s and 1990s, showing huge energy and charisma in her live acts even when she was approaching 80. She died on July 16, 2003 in her home in New Jersey after a battle against cancer.

The late Celia Cruz has almost 80 albums to her credit and she toured all over the world. Ironically, it is in the mainstream US music industry that she had least success, largely because of conservative attitudes towards Spanish-language lyrics. But more enlightened musicians, such as former Talking Head David Byrne, recognised her talent, and they sang a duet in Jonathan Demme's acclaimed film, *Something Wild*. She also appeared in the film version of *The Mambo Kings*.

Famous for her gaudy stage costumes and passionate vocal intensity, Celia Cruz may have fallen foul of Fidel Castro, but even after her death she remains adored by millions of fans across the world. Her lyrics in a song like *Latinos en Estados Unidos* (Latins of the USA) explain why, she had such a following among today's Latino youth:

> Latins of the USA
> We're almost a nation by now
> We come from America that's
> indian, black and Spanish,
> in our migrant minds
> sometimes there's confusion
> but no one can fool
> our souls or our hearts
> because we constantly dream
> of regaining our rightful place.

F ew countries can claim a cultural form as confidently as Trinidad and Tobago can claim calypso. This musical genre is synonymous with the twin-island state, even if other Caribbean nations such as Barbados have produced top-quality calypsonians. Its roots go back far into the history of slavery, when Africans brought with them a tradition of commentary in song, in which praise or derision were heaped on individuals. This African influence became merged with linguistic and stylistic elements from French, Spanish and English sources, creating a truly Creole musical form. By the end of the eighteenth century, the first 'shantwell' (an English-French construction), one Gros Jean, earned a reputation for entertaining the wealthy planters with his *risqué* improvisations.

In the course of twentieth century, calypso spread throughout the Eastern Caribbean, but its home remains Trinidad. Its key elements remain topicality, humour and satire. As such, performers have often fallen foul of the authorities, especially in colonial times, such as when the British tried to ban calypso in the 1930s as 'profane'. Calypso tends to concentrate on scandal, drawn irresistibly to the alleged corruption or sexual misbehaviour of those in power. As such, it is capable of creating considerable controversy and of articulating popular grievances into a potent form of protest. But the best calypsonians also mock themselves with self-deprecating wit and suggestive innuendo.

# THE MIGHTY SPARROW

## 1935–

### GRENADA

Calypso is also an intensely competitive form of music, for each year performers battle it out for the prizes and honours that coincide with Trinidad's world-famous Carnival. With comically grandiose nicknames like Atilla the Hun or Black Stalin, they launch a particular song each January in the run-up to Carnival. In calypso 'tents' or halls they compete against each other, while radio stations broadcast the best of the year's entries. Eventually one singer takes the title of Calypso Monarch, while the favoured song of a particular Carnival wins the Road March Competition as the melody played by most competing steelbands.

There are several contenders to the title of King of Calypso, but a leading candidate is the Mighty Sparrow, aka Slinger Francisco. Ironically, as one of Trinidad's cultural icons, Sparrow was born in the small fishing village of Grand Roy in Grenada, but at the age of one he accompanied his family to Trinidad, where his father had found work near Port of Spain. At school the young Slinger was singled out for his exceptional singing voice and he was encouraged to join the choir at St Patrick's Church. At that time, calypsos were considered crude and disreputable, and Slinger's religious parents would have disapproved strongly of their son singing them. But at a school concert, so the legend has it, he decided to brave the wrath of his parents and teachers by singing a contemporary calypso, Lord Invader's *The Yankees Invade Trinidad.*

This early performance launched Slinger's career, although he was forced to take menial jobs to supplement the seasonal nature of calypso singing. Learning a great deal from veterans such as Lord Melody and Lord Kitchener, he initially performed at a calypso tent in 1954 under the sobriquet of Little Sparrow. The following year he received a better response for such topical songs as *The High Cost of Living* and *Ode to Princess Margaret*, but it was in 1956 that the renamed Mighty Sparrow broke into the big time with his song *Jean and Dinah*, which was subsequently covered by Harry Belafonte.

Throughout the 1950s, Sparrow's fame and popularity grew at a phenomenal rate, a process that continued into the following decade. As song after song became hits, his voice and distinctive style of social commentary became part of everyday Trinidadian life. These were the years in which Eric Williams's People's National Movement dominated politics, and Sparrow became associated with the political leader and his party. Songs such as *P.A.Y.E.* in 1958 helped to explain why Trinidadians should pay their taxes, for instance, and Williams in return encouraged the Carnival Development Committee. But calypso is not naturally suited to toeing a particular official line, and Sparrow found himself castigating 'Doctor' Williams for broken election promises:

> They raise up the taxi fare
> No, Doctor, no
> And the blasted milk gone up so dear
> No, Doctor, no
> But you must remember
> We support you in September
> You better come good
> Because I have a big piece o'mango wood.

Sparrow's particular forte was his ability to produce acute social commentary in a witty and accessible form, and this continued into the 1970s and 1980s with a series of songs that stressed the importance of education and racial unity and the dangers of drugs and mindless materialism. International acclaim followed his national celebrity, and Sparrow made successful tours in Europe, the US and throughout the Caribbean. He also began to compose and sing about overseas issues, mocking the Ugandan dictator in *Idi Amin* (1978) and recording the downfall of the Shah of Iran in *Wanted Dead or Alive* (1980). In the 1980s, he also began to take a more critical stance towards Trinidad and, in particular, the oil boom that was flooding the country with petro-dollars. *Capitalism Gone Mad* (1983) accurately sums up the frenzy of consumerism and the high price paid by the poor during the 'fete' brought about by the oil boom:

> It's outrageous and insane
> The crazy prices here in Port of Spain . . .
> Where you ever hear a television cost seven thousand dollars?
> Quarter million dollars for a piece of land
> A pair of sneakers two hundred dollars

> Eighty to ninety thousand dollars for motor cars
> At last here in Trinidad we see capitalism gone mad . . .

To date, the Mighty Sparrow has won a dozen Calypso Monarch titles and has triumphed in the Carnival Road March competition eight times (second only to Lord Kitchener). In the 1990s, he was still producing songs at an astonishing rate, covering such issues as violence against women, the struggle for democracy in Haiti and criminal violence in Trinidad. In total he has produced some 70 albums, many of them becoming international best-sellers. Keeping up with musical trends, Sparrow has also recorded and performed in the more upbeat, brass section-driven, dance-oriented soca style with songs such as *Soca Pressure* (1985).

In his long career, the Mighty Sparrow has contributed significantly to two major trends in calypso and Trinidadian music in general. His injection of more complex and socially relevant lyrics has helped to move calypso away from its more rudimentary contents towards an outward-looking form of commentary on world affairs. Secondly, his prolific recording has led to the music being known much further afield than in Trinidad and Tobago and the Caribbean in general. As a result, what might have remained an insular, locally appreciated cultural form has grown in international stature, reflecting not only on the innovative Mighty Sparrow himself, but on the creativity of Trinidadian popular culture as a whole.

# BOB MARLEY
## 1945–1981
### JAMAICA

The sprawling slums of West Kingston belie the holiday image of Jamaica. Huge expanses of wooden shacks or concrete tenements are home to hundreds of thousands of the island's poorest people, deprived of basic services and often living on the very edge of survival. Places like Trench Town have grown enormously since the middle of the twentieth century, receiving legions of rural immigrants who came in search of work and 'bright lights' in Kingston. The ghettos have developed a formidable reputation for crime and violence; tourists are warned to steer well away for fear of running into thieves, drug runners or even the notorious political 'posses' who rule the shanty towns.

But if the 'yard', as this tough inner-city patch is known, has produced no shortage of criminal gangs and gunmen, it has also spawned one of the most original and successful musical forms in the world: reggae. Reggae's roots are firmly in the ghetto, even if the music has reached the four corners of the world. And reggae owes much also to Jamaica's other most distinctive cultural creation, the religion of Rastafari.

For it was here, in Kingston, that the idea of a faraway Ethiopian emperor as a god on earth, of Africa as a place of redemption for suffering black people around the globe, turned into a cult.

Robert Nesta Marley arrived in Trench Town, Kingston, as a teenager. He had been born in a village called Nine Mile, in St Ann Parish on February 6, 1945. His mother, Cedella Booker, was only 18; his father, an English captain named Norval Marley, was 50. He was to see little of his father in future years, and it was his mother who brought him to the city, looking for an escape from rural poverty. Trench Town, so called because the slum was built over Kingston's main sewage ditch, was a challenging place for an incoming youth, but Marley made friends and was nicknamed 'tuff gong' for his ability to ward off aggression from bigger, more aggressive boys. After some rudimentary schooling, he began to train as an apprentice welder.

But music was Bob Marley's obsession. He sang in a church choir, encouraged by his religious mother, and made contact with a young singer named Desmond Dekker (whose song *Israelites* was a big hit in 1969). Through Dekker, Marley met the already established Jimmy Cliff and the record producer, Leslie Kong. Marley persuaded Kong to let him audition at his Beverly Studios, and in 1962 his first single, *Judge Not* was released under the mis-spelt name 'Bob Morley'. The song was a flop and, worse still, Kong apparently refused to pay Marley for his work.

By now Marley was friendly with a talented circle of musicians, including Neville 'Bunny' Livingstone and Peter Macintosh (Tosh). In 1963 they formed a group, the Wailing Wailers, and the following year they released their first single, *Simmer Down*.

Reportedly written to placate Marley's anxious mother, the song was recorded at the legendary Coxsone Dodd's Studio One with backing by the Skatalites. Ska was at the time the music in vogue among Jamaican youth, and the upbeat song quickly reached number one with 70,000 sales.

The success of *Simmer Down* established Marley and his group as a force in Jamaica's highly competitive and sometimes violent popular music industry. After recording several more songs, Marley married his girlfriend Rita Anderson (subsequently to be a star in her own right) and then left for the US, where his mother now lived. After several months working in Delaware, Marley returned to Jamaica and resumed worked with the Wailing Wailers. A dispute over the musical direction of the band led to a split with Coxsone, and the group renamed themselves the Wailers. By now, they had moved on from Ska to a style known as Rock Steady, with the emphasis less on dance hall popularity than on 'conscious' lyrics. It was at this time that Marley's political and religious concerns began to enter into his songs with greater prominence.

The big breakthrough came in London when the Wailers, who were working with Johnny Nash, met Chris Blackwell, the Jamaica-born owner of Island Records. Blackwell immediately signed the group to his label, enabling them to record their first album, *Catch a Fire*, a record which won international acclaim as one of the first widely available collections of reggae songs. Blackwell was able to market Marley as an international star, making the music more compatible to US and European tastes with more emphasis on melody and guitar work and less on bass and drums. A string of huge hits followed, such as *Get Up Stand Up* (1973) and *No Woman No Cry* (1975). When rock superstar Eric Clapton re-recorded *I Shot the Sheriff* and reached number one in the US, it was apparent that Marley had also become an iconic figure.

With the meteoric rise of Marley came problems for the Wailers. Peter Tosh and Bunny Wailer left the group to pursue solo careers, but Marley's success continued unabated with his classic live album and *Rastaman Vibration* (1976). It was in that year that Marley was almost killed in what appeared to be an assassination attempt at his Kingston home. The following year he released *Exodus*, judged by some to be his

*Statue of Bob Marley, Kingston, Jamaica.*

best album and certainly among the best-selling. *Exodus* earned him the ultimate accolade when it was named 'Album of the Century' by *Time* magazine, 18 years after Marley's death.

The revelation in 1977 that Marley had cancer came as a bolt out of the blue. He refused to have treatment, claiming that it would violate his Rastafarian beliefs, and he continued as if nothing was wrong. The One Love Peace Concert, held in Kingston in April 1978, brought the leaders of the warring political parties together on stage in a symbolic act of reconciliation. More albums and a historic performance at Zimbabwe's independence ceremony in 1980 followed.

After the release of *Uprising* that year, the band prepared to tour the US with Stevie Wonder. But suddenly Marley's health failed, and after a resurgence of the cancer was diagnosed he underwent treatment in the US and Germany. He died on May 11, 1981, his funeral ten days later attended by thousands in Jamaica. After his death he was awarded Jamaica's Order of Merit.

Today the legend of Bob Marley remains as strong as ever. Songs such as *Stir it Up* or *One Love* – BBC's song of the millennium – are known throughout the world, while the Rastarianism that he espoused won many converts and sympathisers because of his militantly pro-African, anti-'Babylon' lyrics. It has been argued that other contemporary reggae musicians such as Toots Hibbert were as gifted as Marley, but none other captured an international following with the same mix of commercial appeal and political commitment. In a song like *Redemption Song*, Marley used a mix of poetic imagery and controlled anger in his words to convey the concepts of dispossession, biblical prophesy and revolt that lie at the heart of the Rastafari cult:

> Emancipate yourselves from mental slavery
>
> None but ourselves can free our mind
>
> Have no fear for atomic energy
>
> 'Cause none a them can stop the time
>
> How long shall they kill our prophets
>
> While we stand aside and look
>
> Some say it's just a part of it
>
> We've got to fulfill the book.

In a region marked by mass migration, both legal and illegal, the Dominican Republic is a place that people want to reach – and leave. Every year thousands of Haitians cross the border in search of work in sugar plantations or building sites, adding their numbers to the estimated half million already living in the country. Poverty drives them across the border and often into a life of exploitation and fear, but the alternatives of unemployment and hunger are usually even more fearful.

At the same time, many Dominicans have a single burning ambition: to leave their country and discover new opportunities in the Promised Land of the US. Some achieve this goal legally, patiently awaiting their chance to receive a visa. But for the majority the breakthrough never comes, and some decide to take the ultimate risk and try the notorious route across the Mona Passage to Puerto Rico. Only 70 miles separate the eastern tip of the Dominican Republic from Puerto Rico, but it is a perilous journey, often made in leaky *yolas* or small boats. Many would-be migrants never arrive in Puerto Rico, from where they intend to fly to the US; drownings are common, and there are many reported cases of people killed by sharks.

# JUAN LUIS GUERRA

## 1956–

### DOMINICAN REPUBLIC

In a song released in 1989, the Dominican singer Juan Luis Guerra dramatically evoked the hardships and heroism of such illegal migrants. *Visa para un sueño* (Visa for a Dream) tells the story of a group of migrants, desperate to leave their native land and exposed to all the risks of the Mona Passage crossing. The song ends with the chattering noise of a helicopter, suggesting that the US Coast Guard has foiled their attempt to escape their poverty and hopelessness. When Guerra went to Puerto Rico, he was surprised by the reaction he received from the Dominican migrant community there: 'It's one thing to read about *yolas* and deported illegals in the newspapers. But it was quite another thing when I arrived in Puerto Rico and found myself surrounded by those same people who came up to me and thanked me for the image I had given of them, because I'd presented them as heroes of a sort. That was when I started questioning my role as a singer.'

Intentionally or not, Juan Luis Guerra Seijas has become one of the most important commentators on life in the Dominican Republic, but his primary interest has always been music. Born on July 7, 1956 into a relatively prosperous family in Santo Domingo, he was the youngest of three children whose father had been a professional basketball player. The family lived in the leafy middle-class district of Gazcue, and Juan Luis attended school at the La Salle College, where he sang in the choir. From a very young age, however, he had shown an exceptional interest in and talent for music, a characteristic shared by his parents: 'My house was always a musical house… My father listened to the boleros of Agustín Lara, while my mother loved Italian opera. I was mad about the Beatles although I didn't understand a word of their lyrics.' As a child he performed, singing and playing the guitar, at family gatherings and parties. It was here that he familiarised himself with the traditional rhythms and instrumentation of Dominican music, particularly merengue and bachata.

After studying philosophy and literature in Santo Domingo, Guerra won a scholarship at the National Conservatory to pursue his interest in music. From there a supportive teacher encouraged him to apply for a place at the Berklee School of Music in Boston, which he duly won. At that stage he was determined to become a jazz musician and wanted the formal training that Berklee offered. Yet, the experience of total immersion in US-dominated musical forms merely reinforced Guerra's attachment to his native Dominican music, and when he returned periodically to the Dominican Republic to earn some money to support his studies, he played merengue on TV commercials and at fiestas. At the end of his formal jazz-oriented course, he was faced with a dilemma; to become a professional jazz musician, or to return to the musical influences of his childhood and youth.

On his return from the US, Guerra formed a vocal quartet called 4:40, named after the universal tuning pattern of the A note, 440 Hertz. Comprised of two women and two men, 4:40 recorded an album, *Soplando* in 1984. Compared by many to the jazz-inspired melodies of Manhattan Transfer, the album was a failure and marked the end of Guerra's attempt to fuse commercial jazz with merengue. The next two albums, *Mudanza y acarreo* (1986) and *Mientras más lo pienso, tú* (1988) were much more warmly received, since Guerra had now decided to record his own compositions and to emphasise his merengue roots. But it was with *Ojalá que llueva café* (1989) that Guerra really began to establish a reputation as an original talent. As well as *Visa para un sueño*, the album's highlights include the title track, a song whose yearning lyrics were apparently written by an anonymous peasant farmer:

> I hope it rains coffee
> I hope it rains coffee in the fields
> that there falls a shower of yucca and tea
> from the sky a tub of white cheese
> and to the south, a mountain
> of butter and honey
> oh, oh, oh, oh
> I hope it rains coffee in the fields.

4:40's next album, *Bachata rosa* (1990), was, if anything, an even bigger success. Rising to number one across Latin America and selling a million copies in Spain, it featured not only fast-paced merengue, but haunting ballads based on the traditional bachata. This sentimental genre, used to express the melancholy and bitterness of the rural poor, was not widely known outside the Dominican Republic until Guerra seized on its slow sensuality and adorned it with lush orchestration and harmonies. The effect was revolutionary, especially when combined with Guerra's distinctively nasal delivery and socially conscious lyrics.

*Bachata rosa* established Guerra as an international superstar and the best-selling artist of the Spanish-speaking Caribbean. Two more albums followed, and then Guerra stopped recording and touring, seemingly wanting to concentrate more on his work for an evangelical church. But just as critics were beginning to consider his career finished, Guerra released *Ni es lo mismo ni es lgual* in 1998, a more personal collection of songs, with simpler arrangements and acoustic guitar.

Having popularised merengue and bachata internationally like Bob Marley popularised reggae, Juan Luis Guerra is the most prominent exponent of his country's popular culture. Fusing the frenetic speed of merengue, the langorous rhythm of bachata and the melodic sophistication of jazz, he has introduced millions of music fans to the rich musical heritage of his own country and the wider Caribbean.

# KASSAV
## 1978–
### GUADELOUPE

At the end of the 1970s the word *zouk* was used in the French Antilles to refer to a party or popular evening dance. Thanks to Pierre-Edouard Jean Décimus (PEJD), the term was to have much wider meaning from 1978 onwards, when the story of Kassav and its famous zouk music began in the suburbs of Pointe-à-Pitre, the economic capital of Guadeloupe.

It was in these lively neighbourhoods that PEJD used to listen regularly to *tambouyés*, players of the *ka* or traditional drum who used to come into town from the country on Saturday nights to accompany *gwo ka* dancers and singers in the market place. At the age of fifteen he started playing percussion in one of the last great ballroom orchestras. Influenced by these musicians, who were all much older than him, PEJD immersed himself in all the Caribbean rhythms of the postwar years.

As early as 1963 a growing number of night clubs and *pick-ups* (sound systems) as well as the emergence of the *yéyé era* (the French version of 1960s rock 'n' roll) led to the rapid disappearance of the big bands that had catered to an older audience. In the meantime, in the neighbourhoods of Pointe-à-Pitre young musicians were dreaming of the modern instruments pictured on records coming from the United States or Europe. Since they could not afford them, PEJD and his friends were making their own 'slimline' guitars to learn how to play. In 1966, a crooner called Fred Aucagos came back from Paris with a real electric guitar and a sound system equipped with an 'artificial reverb'. With three musicians who liked rock 'n' roll and *yéyé* as much as he did, he founded his first band. 'The Vikings' were mostly composed of young musicians from underprivileged neighbourhoods who supported Red Star, one of the town's main football teams.

Invited a few months later by his friend and neighbour, guitarist Guy Jacquet, PEJD joined The Vikings, first as percussionist, then as drummer, before becoming the band's bass player. Soon afterwards, Camille Sopran, one of the most talented West Indian saxophonists of the time, also joined the band. For the next 12 years this trio made up the basic lineup of The Vikings.

With their modern instruments and beautiful melodies, the musicians delighted the island's youth and became the pride of their neighbourhood. For a decade or more they experienced enormous success, not just in Guadeloupe, but much further afield. In 1970 The Vikings were the first Guadeloupean band since the end of the Second World War to travel to Paris, where they performed in front of 15,000 people.

The tumultuous events of May 1967 in Guadeloupe, the 1968 Paris 'revolution' and the general political situation in the Caribbean all led PEJD to give serious consideration to the status of Guadeloupe and the region in general. By 1969 he had become a professional musician with a passion for electronics. He wrote many songs, including *Neg Mawon*, a tribute to the runaway slaves who refused to accept their condition. In 1978 he had completed the songs inspired by these political reflections and could no longer stand the name 'Vikings', which he saw as too far removed from his cultural reality. It was time for him to leave the band. He then met Freddy Marshall, a singer, producer and ardent supporter of Guadeloupe's Carnival, who immediately agreed to collaborate with him on a recording project in honour of the main figures of *gwo ka* and carnival music (Vélo, Senjan, Gus Nabajoth).

PEJD now adopted the pseudonym of Kassav (cassava), chosen because of an accident that had occurred at the age of seven. He had then learnt at his own cost that the juice extracted from the *kamanyok* could be a dangerous poison. At that age it was difficult for him to understand that the same vegetable could feed someone as a delicious cassava cake fillet with coconut, or kill with its poisonous juice.

In 1970 PJED arrived in Paris, with his precious collection of percussion sounds and songs. There, he hired his bother Georges Décimus (Mister Groove) and the arranger Jacob Desvarieux to work on a studio recording. The result was an album, released in

December 1979, entitled *Love and Ka Dance*. The new sound of Guadeloupean music, zouk, was born.

From 1980 to 1984, to strengthen this innovative musical trend, Georges, Jacob and PJED made several albums under different names: NSI – 'New Sound of the Islands, *Soukwe Kô*, Patrick Saint-Eloi, Jocelyn Moka, Jacob Descarieux, Georges Décimus . . . The strategy bore fruit. Long before the records under the name of Kassav, the album Soukwe Kô, *Christmas and Carnival in the Antilles* was a great success, with 80,000 copies sold.

The mythic *Zouk la sé sel médikamen nou ni* (Zouk is our only medicine) by Georges Décimus and Jacob Desvarieux, won the band its first Gold Record in 1985 for an album whose Guadeloupean sound was only in Creole. The event was celebrated by a concert in Guadeloupe that attracted over 40,000 people. From that moment on, the gates of national and international success were open for Kassav. The French press was surprised to see, for instance, a Caribbean band fill the Zenith venue in Paris, a huge concert hall normally devoted to French pop, without any help from the local media.

The exceptional camaraderie that existed in this band comprised of Guadeloupeans, Martinicans, people from France, an Armenian, an Algerian, an African and a Belgian enabled Kassav to convey an intense *joie de vivre* to their audiences. Solo albums recored by other members of the group – singer Jocelyne Béroard, song writer Patrick Saint-Eloi, Jean-Philippe Marthély (Mr Dynamite on stage) – were as successful as those released under Kassav's name. And within the repertory were endless popular hits which the audience could sing along with during concerts.

Tours continued to expand the band's popularity. In 1987 Kassav performed at the Zenith again, but this time sold out ten consecutive nights. Several recording companies vied to sign the group. CBS (Sony Music) was chosen to produce *Majestik Zouk*, which went Gold within a fortnight. Kassav was then awarded a Platinum Record on the occasion of their tenth anniversary in 1989. With a long list of world tours, Gold and Platinum Records and countless honours, Kassav draws bigger audiences abroad than any other French band. Kassav's songs have also been recorded by famous foreign artists – in the Dominican Republic, Haiti, Mexico, Venezuela and Africa.

In 1991, to avoid endangering the band's future, PEJD and his brother Georges Décimus left Kassav in order to explore new musical avenues, but nevertheless remained close to the other musicians.

In 1999 Kassav celebrated its twentieth anniversary. Through four sold-out concerts in Paris and the Caribbean, more than 40,000 fans showed their attachment to a band that is the pride of a whole generation of music lovers.

# FIELDS OF DREAMS

**Roberto Clemente**

(Puerto Rico)

**Sir Garfield Sobers**

(Barbados)

**Teófilo Stevenson**

(Cuba)

**Merlene Ottey**

(Jamaica)

**Roger Bambuck**

(Guadeloupe)

**Marie-Jose Pérec**

(Guadeloupe)

**Laura Flessel-Colovic**

(Guadeloupe)

In sporting terms the often tiny nations of the Caribbean are giants. An analysis of the 2000 Sydney Olympics revealed that if all the medals won by athletes from the region were combined, the Caribbean would rank sixth in the world. For an area whose total population barely exceeds 35 million (of whom 11 million are Cubans) this is an astonishing achievement. All the more so because much of the Caribbean, Cuba apart, does not have the sporting infrastructure and facilities enjoyed by athletes from other, richer, parts of the world. The success was repeated in the 2004 Athens Olympics when Cuba won 27 medals (including nine golds), Jamaica five medals, the Bahamas two, and the Dominican Republic and Trinidad and Tobago one apiece.

Sport has always been a way for young people from the region to rise above the limitations of their background, to escape poverty and lack of opportunity. Many a would-be boxer, baseball player or cricketer has dreamed of finding fame and wealth through a mixture of natural skill and dedication. And in some cases that dream has come true. A considerable number of Puerto Ricans and Dominicans, for instance, have attained celebrity status in the United States as Major League baseball players. Among the first was Roberto Clemente from Puerto Rico, but today's superstar is Dominican Sammy Sosa, who like many others grew up in poverty around the sugarcane town of San Pedro de Macorís.

Among the French islands, Guadeloupe has a well-deserved reputation in the field of sports, particularly in athletics and football. As early as 1936, Maurice Carlton became the first Guadeloupean to take part in the Olympic Games, finishing fourth in the 100 metres series in Berlin. The champion, of course, was Jessie Owens. Twenty-five years later in 1960, Marlène Canguio became French champion in the junior 80-meter hurdles and 4x100 meter relay event. A semifinalist in the European Championships, she took part in the 1964 Tokyo Olympics.

With the setting up of the Guadeloupean Football League in 1952, the Athletics League in 1960 and the Centre Régional d'Education Physique and Sportive in 1965, Guadeloupe has had the infrastructure and facilities to encourage several outstanding generations of sportsmen and women. During the 1998 World Cup in Paris, hundreds of millions of spectators discovered the talent of Guadeloupe-born Lilian Thuram and Guadeloupe-descended Thierry Henry, who went on to win the European Championship with France in 2000. Thierry plays with Arsenal, where he has been leading scorer, while Thuram plays in Italy with Juventus. And long before them, Guadeloupean Marius Trésor captained France in 1978, considered the best contemporary French player and one of the world's best defenders after the 'Kaiser' Franz Beckenbauer.

In the English-speaking Caribbean, cricket has often been a passport to success. Dating from the era of the Napoleonic Wars when British troops brought the sport with them, cricket was enthusiastically adopted by Caribbean players, and in 1906 the earliest first-class game between a West Indies team and an English side took place. Since then, the region has been home to some of the world's most successful and often flamboyant teams. Sir Garfield Sobers is generally recognised as one of the greatest players of all time, but a list of world-class cricketers would also include such names as Frank Worrell (Barbados), George Headley (Jamaica), Viv Richards (Antigua) and Brian Lara (Trinidad and Tobago). Even a brief visit to any English-speaking island provides reassurance that this tradition is alive and well, as young players practise, often with makeshift bat and wicket, on any available piece of ground.

If baseball and cricket mark the dividing line between Spanish and English speaking territories, then football is the unifying factor. Almost every Caribbean nation is passionate about football, especially when it comes to international matches with other teams from the region. The Caribbean/Central America qualifying games for the World Cup are often among the most hotly contested, with teams like Jamaica or Trinidad and Tobago pitted against those from Honduras or Guatemala. In the World

Cup finals themselves, both Haiti (1974) and Jamaica (1998) acquitted themselves honourably. The highlight of Haiti's campaign was when striker Manno Sanon scored against the legendary Italian goalkeeper Dino Zoff (although the Italians eventually won 3-1), while Jamaica won a memorable victory over Japan.

But perhaps the most important and unexpected Caribbean contribution to football history came in June 1950, when the seemingly impregnable England team were beaten 1-0 in Belo Horizonte, Brazil, by eleven semi-professional players from the US. The scorer of the historic goal, Joe Gaetjens, was in fact a Haitian citizen, and his header led to one of the World Cup's greatest ever shocks. Gaetjens, however, later returned to Haiti, where in 1964 he was arrested by 'Papa Doc' Duvalier's notorious Tontons Macoutes, allegedly for opposing the dictatorship. He was never seen again.

Caribbean-born footballers have also made an impact by playing abroad for professional teams. John Barnes, born in Jamaica, was for many years one of the best-known and respected players in Britain, playing for Watford, Liverpool and Newcastle before choosing a managerial and media career. More recently, Dwight Yorke and Shaka Hislop, both from Trinidad and Tobago, have become regulars at Birmingham City and Portsmouth.

There are many other sports at which Caribbean men and women excel, not least athletics, in which names such as Jamaica's Herb McKenley (finalist in three sprint events in 1952) and Merlene Ottey (eight times an Olympic medallist) stand out. In Athens the women's 4 x 100m relay was won by runners from Jamaica, while the Dominican Republic's Felix Sánchez won a gold medal in the men's 400m hurdles. Cuba continues to wield an influence in the Olympics out of all proportion with its size and population, winning medals in judo, shooting and wrestling as well as eight awards for boxing.

The dominance of Cuban sport reveals what could be achieved elsewhere with greater state support and training. The famous refusal of boxer Teófilo Stevenson to accept the financial benefits of going professional also reveals that the true ethos of sportsmanship can survive the pressures of big business. In this sense, of course, Cuba stands alone in its rejection of sports commercialisation, but the fact that people across the Caribbean enjoy sport for its own sake rather than for what material rewards it might bring is proof that the region's sporting future remains healthy.

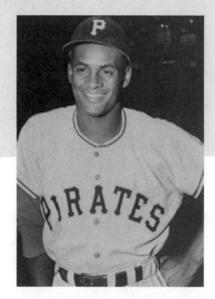

# ROBERTO CLEMENTE

## 1934–1972

### PUERTO RICO

Of all the cultural divides that separate the countries of the Caribbean sport provides one of the deepest. Most nations play football, some with an extraordinary degree of success internationally, but the great dividing line is between those that play cricket and those who play baseball. Colonialism, of course, explains the English-speaking Caribbean's affection for cricket, which often its teams play better than the former colonial power. But baseball remains more of a mystery. Why did the Spanish-speaking countries of the Caribbean and Central America adopt this American sport with such enthusiasm, and why do places like the Dominican Republic and Puerto Rico produce so many world-class players?

Baseball's adoption in the Caribbean is normally traced back to US military occupations – of Puerto Rico and Cuba in 1898 and the Dominican Republic in 1916 – although some believe that the game was introduced earlier by American merchants and sailors. In any event, the sport caught on and local youths were soon forming teams that could compete with the American occupiers. Significantly, baseball, like boxing, soon came to be seen as a way of escaping poverty, as a route to fame and wealth abroad. Young boys from the poorest *barrios* would often practise on waste ground with sugarcane stems for bats and balls made out of green oranges. If they were lucky, they might eventually be spotted by a *buscón* or talent scout working for a big local team or, better still, a US club.

The struggle to achieve recognition, to make it in the US Major Leagues, has bred a certain toughness, even selfishness among those players who are in the competition. It is not uncommon, for example, for successful professionals to return to their homeland with the aim of flaunting their wealth. Humble origins may explain why many feel the need to show off their success. But arguably the Caribbean's finest baseball player – Roberto Clemente of Puerto Rico – was not cast in that mould. His sporting skills, instead, were matched by his humanitarianism, by an instinctive desire to help others as well as by natural flair.

Clemente was born on August 18, 1934 in Barrio San Antón, Carolina, not far from San Juan. The youngest of seven children, as an adolescent he helped his father, a foreman on a sugar plantation and a shopkeeper, load and unload trucks. He was an accomplished athlete, but his real love was baseball which he played from an early age, squeezing a rubber ball for hours on end to build up the muscles in his throwing arm. His talents were noticed while he was still at high school, and at the age of 18 he signed for Santurce, a professional team in the Puerto Rican league. The following year a scout from the Brooklyn Dodgers spotted Clemente at a trial and offered him a

$10,000 bonus to join his team. After finishing high school, Clemente signed with the Dodgers, having turned down better offers from other clubs on the grounds that he had already made a commitment.

After playing with the Dodgers Minor League team and the affiliated Montreal Royals, Clemente was signed by the Pittsburgh Pirates in November 1954. Although only 20 and barely able to speak English, the talented Clemente found himself playing at the highest level. He was not an immediate success, however. The Pirates were in poor form and he suffered from a recurring back problem. But gradually the Pirates built a winning side and in 1960 they won the National League pennant, going on to defeat the New York Yankees in the World Series. That year he also qualified for the first time for inclusion in the All-Star team.

Throughout the 1960s Clemente became a household name among baseball fans nationally, developing into one of the greatest outfielders in the sport's history. He was the National League batting champion in 1961, 1964, 1965 and 1967 and was voted the League's 'most valuable player' in 1966. He also played a key part in the Pittsburgh Pirates second World Series victory in 1971. The sports journalist Larry Schwartz describes his playing as follows:

> At bat, Clemente seemed uncomfortable, rolling his neck and stretching his back. But it was the pitchers who felt the pain. Standing deep in the box, the right-handed hitter would drive the ball to all fields. After batting above .300 just once in his first five seasons, Clemente came into his own as a hitter. Starting in 1960, he batted above .311 in 12 of his final 13 seasons, and he won four batting titles in a seven-year period. He was the 11th player to achieve 3,000 hits. He hit safely in all 14 World Series games he played, helping the Pirates win both seven-game Series.

In 1971, at the age of 37, Clemente was probably at the height of his sporting abilities. The *New Yorker* reported that he played 'something close to the level of absolute perfection . . . as if it were a form of punishment for everyone else on the field.'

During the winter of 1972 Clemente began work on what was to become the Roberto Clemente Sports City in his native Carolina. Wishing to help other Puerto Ricans towards sporting excellence, he donated time and money to the project. He had also ensured that his three sons were all born in Puerto Rico, wanting them, like him, to be proud of their Hispanic heritage. Then, on December 23, news came through that a massive earthquake had devastated the Nicaraguan capital of Manila. Not only were thousands dead and many more left homeless, but reports suggested that the Nicaraguan government was unable or unwilling to distribute relief supplies. Indignant at this news, Clemente decided to act and organised a plane load of supplies for the earthquake victims. On New Year's Eve he and four others boarded an overloaded and ancient DC-7, bound for Managua. Within minutes of takeoff the plane had crashed into the sea off San Juan. It was never found.

Roberto Clemente's final act was typical of his mix of altruism and bravura. When he heard that the Nicaraguan disaster aid was being diverted, he reportedly proclaimed that nobody would steal from Roberto Clemente. While his daring had earned him acclaim as a baseball player, it was ultimately to cost him his life. After a three-day period of mourning in Puerto Rico, Clemente was admitted the following year into the Baseball Hall of Fame when journalists waived the mandatory five-year waiting period. He was the first Hispanic player to receive the honour.

It was Saturday, August 31, 1968, a run-of-the-mill English county cricket match between Nottinghamshire and Glamorgan at Trent Bridge. As Glamorgan bowler Malcolm Nash looked at the facing batsman, he could not have imagined that he was about to feature in a world record-breaking cricket event. As he bowled the first ball of the over, the batsman struck it for six runs. And the next. And the next. And two more. Finally, as Nash delivered the last ball of the over, the batsman stepped forward and hit it clean out of the ground. Six sixes in a first-class game. It was a first, never yet to have been repeated, and often shown on television as one of cricket's most extraordinary moments. Legend has it that the last ball to be hit out of the ground was not found until the following Monday, when it was still running down the hill!

# SIR GARFIELD SOBERS

## 1936 –

### BARBADOS

The batsman's name was Garfield St Aubrun Sobers, better known as Garry Sobers, a 32-year-old Barbadian, who was already considered one of the finest all-rounders in the game. He was born in Bay Land, Bridgetown, the fifth of six children in a working-class family. His father, a merchant seaman, died as a victim of a German torpedo when Garfield was only six. From an early age, it seems, cricket was in his blood. With his brother, Gerald, he helped their local primary school to win the national championship for three consecutive years. By the age of 13 he was playing at a senior level, and three years later he was recruited into the island's Police First Division eleven. At 17, he made his international debut for the West Indies against a touring English side in Jamaica.

Sobers's career is comprised of superlative statistics and path-breaking achievements. In 1958, for instance, he set a record at the age of 21 by scoring 365 runs not out in a Test match. This feat was not matched for 36 years, until Brian Lara scored 375 in 1994 at a Test match in Antigua. Another high point occurred at Lord's, London, in 1966, when Sobers and David Holford withstood an onslaught of English bowling to score 163 and 105 not out respectively. In total, Sobers batted 160 innings in 93 Tests, scoring no fewer than 8,032 runs at the highest level, producing an innings average of 57.8 runs.

But Sobers was not only a superlative batsman, he was also a devastating bowler. Left-handed, he had a wide repertoire of bowling styles, ranging from medium-fast to deceptive googlies. In his Test career he took 235 wickets, at an average of 34 runs made per wicket. His best ever score was six wickets for 73 runs. As if this was not enough, Sobers also took 109 catches in 93 Test matches for the West Indies, in itself a remarkable achievement. No wonder that C.L.R. James, the intellectual connoisseur of Caribbean cricket, described him as 'this superb product of the modern age'.

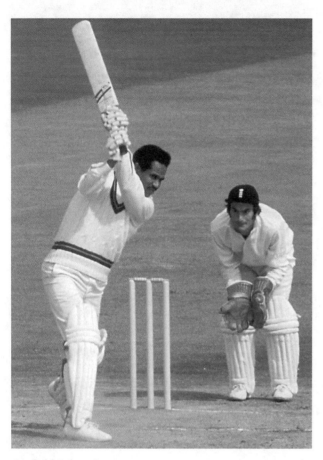

*Garfield Sobers in action*

Sobers's career stretched across two decades. He played for Barbados and the West Indies between 1953 and 1974, for South Australia between 1961 and 1964, and for Nottinghamshire between 1968 and 1974. Until his retirement from the game in 1974 he also played in countless celebrity and charity matches. While in Australia he set a double record of 1,000 runs and 50 wickets in a single season.

Yet despite these virtuoso displays, Sobers was not the product of a conventional coaching regime. According to Ian Wooldridge in *Wisden Cricketers' Almanac*:

Perhaps the most fundamental argument against the modern idiom of cricket is that Sobers was never coached. He mistrusted coaches. He learned the game playing all the spare hours in the street with his brothers and friends and then, after the early Barbados sunset, playing on with miniature implements, much to the detriment of the furniture, in his despairing mother's house.

Sobers's instinctive approach to the game also involved a desire to play attacking, entertaining cricket. He was much less interested in defensive strategies, in playing for a draw, than in going all out for a heroic victory. Sometimes this attitude won him glory; on other occasions, he incurred the wrath of those who felt that caution would have brought about a better result. Sobers took chances in order to make games more interesting for the spectator and, as a result, sometimes lost. In 1968, for example, when captaining the West Indies team against England, he declared when his side was 92 for 2 in its second innings. With a West Indies first innings of lead of 122, Sobers calculated that England had a remote chance of catching up if his side declared and – more importantly – that it would make for an exciting match. England did indeed catch up, and Sobers came close to losing the captaincy. In the next Test he responded as he knew best to his critics by scoring 152 and 95 not out as well as taking three wickets in each innings.

Often unconventional and never boring, Sobers was also a courageous and sporting player. He refused to wear much of the protective equipment of modern cricket, appearing informal and even nonchalant at times. He suffered few injuries (interestingly, his worst sporting injury came when playing as a goalkeeper in the Barbados national side, an incident that may have hastened his retirement with cartilage problems). He never questioned an umpire's decision and was even known to start walking back towards the pavilion before he had been officially dismissed.

Perhaps Sobers's one failing during his career was his decision to play and coach in Rhodesia (now Zimbabwe) in 1969, a decision that led to charges of collaborating with *apartheid*. He later looked back on the episode with regret, but at the time he was heavily criticised in the Caribbean and beyond for appearing to condone racism. His attitude was that he was seeking to advance the cause of racial integration by coaching black, as well as white, boys.

Shortly after his retirement, Sobers was knighted in February 1975 by the Queen at the Garrison Racecourse in Bridgetown. The ceremony took place barely a mile from his humble childhood home. He had already been honoured by appearing on a special postage stamp to commemorate Barbados's independence in 1966. In 1998 he was named a National hero of Barbados, joining such luminaries as Grantley Adams and Errol Barrow. But perhaps the greatest tribute came a decade earlier when Sir Donald Bradman conferred on Sobers the title of the greatest all-rounder he had ever seen. Anybody who can remember Sobers's classic performances – or who sees the re-run footage of that day at Trent Bridge, Nottinghamshire – would find it hard to dispute such a judgment.

*Garfield Sobers being knighted, 1975*

# TEÓFILO STEVENSON

## 1952 –

CUBA

Like sportsmen anywhere else in the world, boxers in the Caribbean see their sport as a rapid but precarious route out of poverty. The dream of many young fighters is to turn professional, to hit a winning and streak and to make it in the United States, where the real money lies. In every city in the Caribbean there is at least one boxing club, where young men train fanatically with this aim in mind. And because boxing is one sport in which blacks have traditionally been encouraged to excel, the lure for black Caribbean-born boxers is all the stronger as they consider the success and fame of figures such as Muhammad Ali or Mike Tyson.

But in Cuba, home to many of the region's most feared boxers, the dreams and ambitions are necessarily different. Professional boxing was banned by the revolutionary government in 1961, putting an end to a business through which gambling and Mafia activity had long flourished. With an influx of aid and advice from the Eastern bloc communist countries the regime attempted to change the culture of boxing, developing both an amateur ethos and a commitment to excellence. Cuban boxing became a force to be reckoned with in the 1960s, with expertise provided by Soviet coaching staff, and by the early 1970s it had produced one of the all-time great fighters: Teófilo Stevenson.

Stevenson's father had migrated to Cuba in 1923 in an attempt to escape the economic crisis and unemployment devastating his native island of St Vincent. After working on a sugar plantation, as a stevedore and a teacher of English, he discovered that he was a natural boxer. His career was as short as it was brilliant, however; when he realised that local promoters were paying him only ten pesos to take on formidable heavyweights, he gave up, unbeaten in seven fights.

Teófilo Stevenson was born near Camagüey in 1952. An energetic and often mischievous child by all accounts, he found an outlet for his aggression in the local gym. His height and strength caught the attention of a local trainer, but Stevenson was forced to train in secret, fearful of his parents' disapproval. Eventually, however, he was forced to admit that he was boxing on a regular basis and, with his parents' grudging consent, he became involved in the Cuban post-revolutionary sports system, winning a junior title and then the national youth title in 1968. The following year he made it to the final of the national senior heavyweight contest, but lost. In the crowd, however, was the Soviet coach who was in charge of building the Cuban team for the 1972 Olympics. He liked what he saw of the tall youngster from Camagüey.

After a series of mixed results, Stevenson began to grow in boxing stature, perfecting his jab and working on his mighty knockout punch. At the 1972 Olympics in Munich the 20-year-old Cuban was an almost unknown, but immediately he made an impact.

After knocking out the Pole, Ludwik Denderys, Stevenson faced the American Duane Bobick in a fight full of political overtones. Stevenson won again, delighting nationalistic Cuban supporters and scoring a major propaganda blow. He then defeated the German favourite before winning the gold medal when his Romanian opponent withdrew with a broken thumb. It was the first gold that Cuba had won since 1904.

Four years later in Montreal, Stevenson was in even more devastating form, taking just seven minutes and 22 seconds to demolish his first three opponents. In the final he faced another Romanian, who spent two rounds trying to escape Stevenson's right hook before being knocked down in the third round.

It was a similar story in Moscow in 1980, but here at last an opponent managed to last all three rounds. In the semi-final, the Hungarian Istvan Leval reportedly jumped for joy when he heard the final bell ring, even though it was obvious that he had lost the fight. Just to survive the full three rounds with Stevenson was considered a significant victory! In the final the Cuban went on to beat the Russian Pyotr Zayev, thereby setting a world record by winning three Olympic golds in one division.

Could he have gone on to win a fourth? We shall never know, as in 1984 the Soviet Union and its allies, including Cuba, boycotted the Olympic Games in Los Angeles. Around that time, Stevenson's career seemed to decline somewhat and he was defeated several times between 1984 and 1986. Finally, after a brief recovery of winning form in 1986, he retired at the age of thirty-four. As the state newspaper, *Granma*, accurately commented: 'The pressure of being at the top meant that he couldn't keep getting back to the level at which he had operated for so long. It had taken its toll. But he went out in a blaze of glory and in the certain knowledge that he is the greatest amateur boxer of all time.'

'Boxers in Cuba begin to prepare while they're still in the womb,' Stevenson once said. But apart from his natural skill and stamina, there is another attribute that has singled him out for a special sort of adulation in his native Cuba. From 1972 onwards professional boxing promoters recognised Stevenson's crowd-pulling potential and began to besiege him whenever he travelled abroad with lucrative offers to turn professional. After Don King had reportedly offered him several million dollars to turn professional, Stevenson went on record to reject the offer and all that it implied:

> Professional boxing treats a fighter like a commodity to be bought and sold and discarded when he is no longer of use. I wouldn't exchange my piece of Cuba for all the money they could give me.

Sceptics point out that the Cuban state has rewarded Stevenson for his loyalty with houses, cars and a regular salary as a boxing consultant to the national sports institute. For this it can enjoy the puzzlement and disappointment felt by the US boxing industry that a fighter would turn down millions of dollars on principle.

Teófilo Stevenson has remained a controversial figure and a thorn in the flesh of the American authorities. In 1998 he led the Cuban team's walkout from the Houston world championships, enraged at some dubious refereeing decisions. The following

*Professional boxing treats a fighter like a commodity to be bought and sold and discarded when he is no longer of use. I wouldn't exchange my piece of Cuba for all the money they could give me.*

year he was briefly arrested at Miami airport after head-butting an airline worker, who, he claimed, had insulted Cuba. Meanwhile, Cuban boxing goes from strength to strength. At the Sydney Olympics in September 2000, Felix Savon, with whom Stevenson sparred and fought, emulated his predecessor's achievement by winning a third consecutive gold medal in the heavyweight division. He, too, has refused to turn professional. In Athens no fewer than five Cuban boxers won gold medals, with a further two silvers and a bronze.

Over the last two decades Jamaicans have made a name for themselves in almost every conceivable area of sport. Leaving aside the traditional field of cricket, the island has produced world-class competitors in football (the 'Reggae Boyz' endeared themselves to many during the 1998 World Cup finals in France), netball (the island is ranked fifth in the world) and boxing. Perhaps most bizarrely, Jamaica entered a bobsled team in the 1992 Winter Olympics in France. Although the four Jamaicans finished 34th in the event, their extraordinary adventure inspired the film *Cool Runnings* – a fitting tribute to a team from an island that never sees snow.

But it is perhaps in athletics that Jamaica has most successfully distinguished itself. Since 1948 Jamaicans have won many Olympic medals, with the sprinter Herb McKenley taking three medals at the 1952 Olympics, including a gold for his part in the 1600m relay. Also in that winning relay team was Arthur Wint, another multi-medal runner. More recently, Deon Hemmings won the island's first female event gold medal in 1996, while at Sydney in 2000 Jamaica won several track and field medals.

# MERLENE OTTEY
## 1960 –
### JAMAICA

Why are Jamaicans so good at running? It has been suggested – only half-seriously – that many children who go to school in rural areas are natural athletes from an early age as they often have to run several miles from home to school, especially when late. A more plausible explanation is that athletics, and sport in general, is very well organised at a school, regional and national level and that precocious talent is quickly spotted and nurtured. There is intense competition for places in Jamaica's athletics teams, and the races to qualify for inclusion can be as gruelling as the international events themselves.

If Jamaica has been home to many top-class athletes over the years, few can hope to equal the records set by Merlene Ottey, who at the age of 40 was still competing at the Sydney Olympics. There she won a silver medal for her part in the 4 x 100m female relay race. This was achieved despite a highly controversial ban for allegedly using the anabolic steroid nandrolene and a subsequent clearance by the International Amateur Athletic Federation. Little wonder that supporters and competitors alike were astonished at the resilience and stamina of an athlete who has been called the greatest female sprinter in history. Tall, graceful, and above all extremely fast, Ottey could still outrun athletes half her age.

Merlene Ottey was born on May 10, 1960 in the small rural community of Cold Spring in the parish of Hanover. The fourth of seven children, she attended local schools, where her athletic ability was soon detected. At high school in the 1970s she developed her ambition to become a runner, inspired, she says, by listening to radio broadcasts of the 1976 Montreal Olympics, where Jamaican Donald Quarrie qualified

*Merlene Ottey celebrates after a race*

*It's been tough, and mentally it was difficult to focus, but now I have some time before the Olympics and I'm going to train hard and have a try . . . I'm keen just to run, just to get back in the race.*

for the sprint final. In her teens she competed in national and regional competitions, registering a time of 25.9 seconds for the 200m at the age of fifteen. The previous year, however, her debut had been altogether less promising, when in her first official race at a local high school she finished last! In 1978 she won gold and bronze medals in sprint and relay events for Jamaica at the Junior Central American and Caribbean Championships. The following year, she represented Jamaica at the Pan American Games in Puerto Rico, winning a bronze medal in the 200m.

1979 was also the year in which Ottey took up a place at the University of Nebraska in the United States. Like many other sportsmen and women, she recognised that she required a larger international stage than that offered by Jamaica and access to top-class training and coaching facilities. It was there that her talent really blossomed. From 1979 to 1984 she won a series of races, both indoor and outdoor, beginning with the Moscow Olympic Games of 1980. There she won a bronze in the 200m, with a formidable time of 22.20 seconds. Over the next few years, Ottey was rarely out of the public eye, setting several US collegiate records and even a world record in the 300m sprint. At one point in 1982, she held the record for nine out of the ten best recorded times for the 300m.

In 1984 Merlene Ottey was again selected to run for Jamaica in the Olympic Games, this time held in Los Angeles. On this occasion, she won two bronze medals, one for the 100m and the other for the 200m. The following year, she won two golds at the Central American and Caribbean Championships. Although Ottey finished only fourth in the 1988 Olympic Games, the 1980s were marked by a succession of victories and titles at other world-class events. Between September 1987 and August 1991, for instance, she ran 57 100m races and won all of them.

But the 1990s perhaps marked the peak of Ottey's remarkable running career. After taking silver medals in World Championship races in 1993 and 1995, she again represented Jamaica – at the age of 36 – at the 1996 Olympic Games at Atlanta. Here she won two silver medals and a bronze, coming second in the 100m and 200m and third in the 4 x 100m relay. It is almost impossible to come any closer to winning a gold than Ottey did in the 100m final. She lost by the tiniest recordable time of .005 seconds, having previously failed to win the 1993 World Championship by a similar margin.

As a result, Merlene Ottey, with six individual and two team medals, is the most medalled sportsperson never to have won a gold at the Olympics. The last of these awards was gained at Sydney, when after finishing fourth in the 100m final, she contributed to Jamaica's silver medal in the 4 x 100m. She also holds a record 14 medals from World Championships.

The later part of Ottey's career was unfortunately overshadowed by controversy when in July 1999 she was accused of taking the banned substance nandrolene – a charge she vehemently denied – and was banned. But this decision was overturned almost a year later. She remarked:

> It's been tough, and mentally it was difficult to focus, but now I have some time before the Olympics and I'm going to train hard and have a try . . . I'm keen just to run, just to get back in the race.

Her part in Jamaica's relay success was evidence of that determination and proof of her ability to overcome intense psychological pressure. In recognition of those qualities, Ottey, who was then mostly living in Monte Carlo, was in 1993 appointed honorary ambassador of Jamaica. She appeared at her seventh Olympic Games in Athens, at the age of 44, competing in the colours of her adopted Slovenia, but although her time in the 100m qualifying heat was the second fastest, she failed to collect a medal, being eliminated in the semi-final with a time of 11.21 seconds.

## Merlene's medal file

### 8 Olympic Medals

**Moscow 1980** – 200m bronze

**Los Angeles 1984** – 100m & 200m bronze

**Barcelonia 1992** – 200m bronze

**Atlanta 1996** – 100m & 200m silver & 4 x 100 relay bronze

**Sydney 2000** – 4 x 100 relay silver

### 14 World Championship Medals

**Helsinki 1983** – 200m silver & 4 x 100 relay bronze

**Rome 1987** – 100m & 200m bronze

**Tokyo 1991** – 4 x 100 relay gold, 100m & 200m bronze

**Stuttgart 1993** – 200m gold, 100m silver & 4 x 100m relay bronze

**Gothenburg 1995** – 200m gold, l00m silver & 4 x 100 relay silver

**Athens 1997** – 200m bronze

# GUADELOUPE'S ATHLETES

The French island of Guadeloupe has given the Caribbean, and the wider world, an extraordinary array of talent, both in football and in athletics. The following three medal-winners, spanning a period from the 1960s to the present day, are just some of the better-known sportsmen and women from Guadeloupe.

**Roger Bambuck** was born on November 22, 1945 in Pointe-à-Pitre. He started his athletics career with the 'Redoubtable' club in 1962 and won the French Schools and Universities Sports Association Championship for 100m in 1963 and 1964. The same year, he was record-holder for the 200m and 4x100m relay. He was barely 20 years old when selected for the French team to take part in the Tokyo 1964 Olympics, where he ran in the semi-final of the 200m.

In July 1965 Bambuck became co-record holder for the 100m, and a year later won the 200m and 4x100m relay at the European Championships, helping to set a new world record in the latter. At the 1968 Mexico Olympics, he took part in no fewer than three finals, coming fifth in the 100m, fifth also in the 200m and winning a bronze in the 4x100m relay. That same year, he broke the world record for the 100m in Sacramento, coming in at 10 seconds, but the record was bettered the same day by Ronnie Ray Smith of the USA.

After finishing his athletics career and having held the French 100m record for two decades, Roger Bambuck studied medicine and then went into politics, serving as Secretary of State at the Ministry of Youth and Sports in Paris between 1988 and 1991.

**Marie-José Pérec** was born in Basse-Terre in 1968, where she started running at the Collège Campenon in 1984. Four years later, she travelled with her mother to Paris, where she caught the eye of national coaches, and that year she represented France in the Olympics in Seoul, running in the 200m. After winning a bronze medal during the 1990 European Championships in Croatia, she went on to win the gold for the 400m in the 1992 Barcelona Olympics, defeating the reigning champion Olha Bryzhina in an exciting final.

After maintaining her winning form in European Championships in Helsinki (1994) and Gothenburg (1995), Perec was favourite to win in the 1996 Atlanta Olympics. She duly triumphed in the 400m final, beating strong competition from Australia and Nigeria, with a time of 48.25 seconds, a new French record, her career best, and the third best performance ever. This victory made her the first athlete of either sex to win the 400m twice in Olympic competitions. Three days later, Pérec made Caribbean history again, beating Jamaica's Merlene Ottey in the 200m final and thereby becoming only the second runner to win golds in the 200m and 400m contests.

Laura Flessel-Colovic was born on November 6, 1971, and at the age of seven abandoned dancing to take up fencing with a club in Pointe-à-Pitre. Rising rapidly through the island's fencing ranks, the left-handed Flessel-Colovic then moved to France in 1990 to concentrate exclusively on training in her discipline, the épée, with the Chantilly Fencing Club.

Her individual list of awards is impressive: two gold medals at the 1996 Atlanta Olympics, a bronze medal at Sydney in 2000, a silver in Athens in 2004, two world champion titles in 1998/1999, a bronze medal at the 1995 World Championships, a European second place in 1993, two French champion medals in 1998 and 2000, and three gold medals in Pan-American Championships in 1991, 1993 and 1994.

Her list of team awards includes the world champion title in 1998, a gold medal at the 1996 Olympics, the world vice-champion title in 1995, a bronze medal in the 1997 World Championships, the 1998 European Club Championship Cup and four French championship titles in 1993, 1994, 1996 and 1999.

Known as *la guêpe* (the wasp) for her fast, aggressive fencing style, Laura Flessel-Colovic has shown that a black woman can reach the top of her chosen sport, a sport normally dominated by white men.

*Laura Flessel-Colovic,* la guêpe

# BIBLIOGRAPHY

Abel, Christopher and Nissa Torrents eds. *José Martí: Revolutionary Democrat*. London: Athlone Press, 1986.

Arthur, Charles and Michael Dash eds. *Libéte: A Haiti Anthology*. Kingston, Jamaica: Ian Randle Publishers, 1999.

Balderrama, Maria R. *Wifredo Lam and his Contemporaries, 1938–1952*. New York: Studio Museum, 1993.

Beckles, Hilary. *A History of Barbados*. Cambridge: Cambridge University Press, 1990.

Bennett, Louise. Selected *Poems. Kingston*, Jamaica: Sangsters, 1982.

Boxer, David and Veerlee Poupeye. *Modern Jamaican Art*. Kingston, Jamaica: Ian Randle Publishers, 1998.

Carpentier, Alejo. *The Kingdom of This World*. New York: Noonday Press, 1989.

Césaire, Aimé. *The Collected Poetry*. Berkeley: University of California, 1984.

Duncan, John. *In the Red Corner: A Journey into Cuban Boxing*. London: Yellow Jersey Press, 2000.

Forrester, Claire and Alvin Campbell. *Merlene Ottey: Unyielding Spirit*. Kingston, Jamaica: West Indies Publishing, 1996.

Galván, Manuel de Jesús. *The Sword and the Cross*. Trans. Robert Graves. Oxford: Macmillan, 2004.

Gottlieb, Karla. *The Mother of Us All: A History of Queen Nanny*. Trenton, NJ: Africa World Press, 2000.

James, C.L.R. *The Black Jacobins: Toussaint L'Ouverture and the San Domingo Revolution*. London: Allison and Busby, 1991.

Lewis, Arthur. *The Theory of Economic Growth*. London: Allen and Unwin, 1955.

Lewis, Gordon. *Puerto Rico: Freedom and Power in the Caribbean*. New York: Monthly Review Press, 1963; Kingston, Jamaica: Ian Randle Publishers, 2004

Lewis, Rupert Charles. *Marcus Garvey: Anti-Colonial Champion*. Trenton, NJ: Africa World Press, 1988.

Maclean, Geoffrey. *An Illustrated Biography of Trinidad's Nineteenth Century Painter Michel Jean Cazabon*. Trinidad: Aquarella Galleries, 1986.

Manley, Michael. *A History of West Indian Cricket*. London: Andre Deutsch, 1995.

Manley, Rachel. *Drumblair*. Kingston, Jamaica: Ian Randle Publishers, 1998.

Manuel, Peter. *Caribbean Currents: From Rumba to Reggae.* Philadelphia: Temple University Press, 1995.

Mason, Peter, *Bachannal! The Carnival Culture of Trinidad.* Kingston, Jamaica: Ian Randle Publishers, 1999.

McKay, Claude. *Banana Bottom.* London: Xpress, 1999.

Naipaul, V.S. *A House for Mr Biswas.* New York: Knopf, 1995.

Ospina, Calvo Hernando. *¡Salsa! Havana Heat, Bronx Beat.* London: Latin America Bureau, 1995.

Payne, Anthony. *Politics in Jamaica. Kingston,* Jamaica: Ian Randle Publishers, 1995.

Poitier, Sidney. *This Life.* London: Hodder & Stoughton, 1980.

Pons, Frank Moya. *The Dominican Republic: A National History.* New York: Hispaniola Books, 1994.

Quirk, Robert E. *Fidel Castro.* New York: W.W. Norton, 1995.

Rodney, Walter. *A History of the Guyanese Working People, 1881–1905.* Baltimore: Johns Hopkins University Press, 1982.

Roumain, Jacques. *Masters of the Dew.* Oxford: Heinemann, 1978.

Sarduy, Pedro Pérez and Jean Stubbs. *Afro-Cuba: An Anthology of Cuban Writing on Race, Politics and Culture.* London: Latin America Bureau, 1993.

Sheppard, Jill. *Marryshow of Grenada: An Introduction.* Barbados: Letchworth Press, 1987.

Smart, Ian Isidore. *Nicolás Guillén: Popular Poet of the Caribbean.* Texas: University of Missouri Press, 1990.

Thomas, John Jacob. *Froudacity: West Indian Fables Explained.* London: New Beacon, 1975.

Walcott, Derek. *Omeros.* New York: Noonday Press, 1992.

Walker, Paul Robert. *Pride of Puerto Rico: The Life of Roberto Clemente.* New York: Harcourt Brace, 1998.

White, Timothy. *Catch a Fire: The Life of Bob Marley.* New York: Owl Books, 1998.

Williams, Eric. *From Columbus to Castro: The History of the Caribbean, 1942–1969.* London: Andre Deutsch, 1970.

Williams, Sheldon. *Voodoo and the Art of Haiti.* London: Morland Lee, 1969.

Worcester, Kent. *C.L.R. James: A Political Biography.* Albany, NY: State University of New York Press, 1996.

# INDEX